A
LANCASHIRE
YEAR

by
Benita Moore, A.L.A.

Carnegie Press 1989

The author would like to thank:

The Lancashire Magazine, The Lancashire Evening Telegraph, Lancashire Libraries/Newsletter , Mrs D McCloney and the staff of Rossendale Libraries, Lancashire County Council.

With special thanks to:

Jennifer Skilliday, Cheryl Wright, Trevor Whitehead, Eric Leaver and anyone else who has helped in any way.

Cartoons by Andrew Parker

A Lancashire Year
Benita Moore

Copyright © Benita Moore 1989

Published by Carnegie Press, 125 Woodplumpton Road, Fulwood, Preston PR2 2LS
Tel: (0772) 728868

Typeset in 10pt Times by Carnegie Press

Printed by T. Snape & Co., Bolton's Court, Preston.

ISBN 0 948789 37 9

Contents

Introduction

This book is based on my experiences whilst working as librarian on the Lancashire County Mobile Library Service some 25 years ago. The library was based at Ramsbottom and we travelled over a very wide area of Lancashire.

This kind of work greatly appealed to me, and the driver and myself met some lovely people and enjoyed the superb scenery and pretty villages along our route.

Although the book is based on my work it should be emphasised that the characters are purely fictitious and any resemblance to any person, living or dead, is accidental.

I hope you enjoy reading this book as much as I have enjoyed re-living a very happy period of my life.

Benita Moore

Biographical Details

Benita Moore lives at Rising Bridge and has been a Librarian for 35 years. She is very interested in local history and particulary in Lancashire folk, indeed anything connected with the county of her birth.

She has had two books published previously, *Gobbin Tales* and *Just Life*, and hopes to continue writing about Lancashire and its traditions and people.

Currently working at Oswaldtwistle Public Library, she is married to videographer Gordon Moore and they have two teenage daughters.

Chapter One

In the beginning

I T WAS on a lovely clear September morning when I drove into the market square at Ramsbottom, a small country town in northern Lancashire. My first impressions were of the pleasant little gardens belonging to the houses in the square, and they gave me a feeling of peace and relaxation which was to be with me throughout the whole of the time I was there.

It was my first morning at my new job as Mobile Librarian for the Ramsbottom Region of the County Library. As I parked the car on the library car park I saw the Mobile Library emerge from its garage round the back. Painted a bright red with cream, it was a good advertisement for itself, as nobody could miss the huge splash of colour as it rolled through the country lanes. Inside the van were some

Market place, Ramsbottom, round the corner from the Central Library

3,000 books which we tried to make as varied and interesting as possible, including not only light novels but books on the more popular subjects as well.

I announced my arrival to Mrs. Burch, the Chief Librarian, who greeted me warmly and explained my duties briefly. It appeared that the library ran on a fortnightly rota, visiting some 20 villages and hamlets in a 20-mile radius. Bill McGregor, the driver, climbed out of the cab and shook my hand. He seemed a friendly man and, as he had been with the Mobile Library since its beginning ten years before, I presumed he would be very useful, and future circumstances proved just how right I was.

We were due at the first stop at 9.35 a.m. so there was no time to lose, and grabbing my lunch I clambered aboard. There was a comfortable seat in front for me to use whilst travelling and a neat little locker for my belongings. At the back of the seat were various cupboards and 2 tables for us to work on. Briefly the system was this: each reader had a ticket with his name, address and stop number (which we allotted) written on it. We took the tickets out of each book and put them in the reader's ticket, then we filed the tickets in order of stop number.

As we passed through the pleasant country lanes and villages on our way to Affetside, the first village of the day, I noticed the lovely autumn colours of the trees and the berries already ripening in the hedges. I thought, how pleasant is the English countryside, even a few miles from industrial towns!

We eventually drew up outside a row of neat whitewashed cottages. Bill blew the horn, and almost at once (or so it seemed to me) several doors flew open and a few women, each with a pile of books, crowded into the van and deposited their books on my table. I sorted the books, and then turned my attention to my 'Readers', as I affectionately called them.

Our readers, (at this stop at any rate) were pretty much of the same type; elderly or middle aged with a fancy for light romances and novels. I offered to help them in their choice of books, but was spurned by tart refusals, or remarks like, 'the other lady told us to read such and such a thing'.

I realised that it would take some time to win their confidence as country people are inclined to be rather rigid, and a change of Librarian was as unpopular as a change of milkman. However, as the same thing happened more or less throughout the morning, I decided to persevere and tried to remain cheerful. After a few visits, however, I was amazed at the change in people's attitude and I was soon deluged by cheerful remarks and even 'private confidences' were related to me by the villagers in whispered tones.

Lunch time was a cheerful affair, the first of many such episodes. At the last stop in the main village, Bill produced his famous teapot, and I soon fell into the routine of going to various houses, waiting whilst they filled our tea-pot and asked, 'Have you milk and sugar?' I enjoyed these little trips to the quaint and scrupulously clean little houses as it gave me a chance to talk to my readers in their own domains, and they were usually pleased to tell me about their homes and families.

On this first day, we had our sandwiches and tea outside the village by the side of a little stream which meandered round the local farms.

'What a charming place,' I remarked to Bill. 'Are all the villages we visit as nice?'

He grinned saying, 'You wait and see, especially when we visit all the farms and hamlets way out, they're a treat.'

Later, as I began to enjoy and look forward to each day, I remembered his words.

After lunch we visited a farm called 'Holly Trees,' just outside the next village. The farmer's wife was just as I imagined one to be, rosy, full-bosomed and with a spotless overall trailing round her gumboots. She mounted the steps, balancing a huge pile of books in her right hand.

'Hello there,' said Bill, 'this is Mrs. Moore our new librarian', indicating me with a nod of the head.

'Pleased to meet you,' said Mrs Jay, 'Can you recommend a good historical novel?'

I duly obliged while Mrs. Jay chatted about her family, the weather, the farm and anything else she could think of. She was a prolific talker, as indeed were many of my future clients, and on days when I had time to spare I had an enjoyable time listening to them, on days when I was very busy, however, I secretly cursed this chit-chat.

On this particular afternoon, we were not 'busy', Bill informed me, so I listened and looked round the neat farmyard with interest. A flock of geese were cackling on a small patch of grass near the window, two black and white collies frisked round the van, and a wide variety of hens scrabbled about the cobbles, altogether a very pleasant scene. But Mrs Jay certainly claimed my attention. She wanted light and historical books for herself, war stories and cowboys for hubby, classics for her daughter, and something on sociology for her son. This was to set the pattern for a large number of readers who regularly chose books for their working families, and we had many strange requests, such as the one for books on 'the origin of fish and chip shops' or 'how many public houses there are in Lancashire'.

The next stop we made was at a group of small cottages just off the main road. Down we went over a very bumpy track, and sure enough, before the horn had finished sounding, doors flew open and several people came into the van. One dear old lady in particular caught my attention. She sported a huge hairnet, which she wore over an untidy collection of steel curlers. As these were all very loosely fastened I wondered what effect if any they would have on her thin grey hair. However, I attended to my work and thought no more about her until she deposited her pile of books on to my desk, together with her top set of dentures which unfortunately bounced onto the floor. I was tempted to laugh, but managed to conceal this by bending down and picking up the offending items and returning them to their owner, who promptly pushed them back into place, much to my amazement! I could see I had a lot to learn about people!

She deposited her pile of books on my desk, together with her bottom set of dentures!

After no further incidents, off we went to the next stop, a charming little cottage by the roadside. The owner of this cottage was a sprightly middle-aged spinster with the delightful name of Marigold Masham. I was enchanted. Names like this have always appealed to me, and when I discovered the name of her cottage was 'Honey Hole' it made my day. We had coffee and scrumptious home-made scones at Miss Masham's and whilst we ate she told us about her two poodles called 'Salt' and 'Pepper', who were ten years old, and her cat 'Ju-Ju', a mere babe of fifteen years. As we drove away to the next stop, I remarked to Bill that

I found all these people very interesting and amusing. He replied that I had many more such people and places to meet yet.

We had to return to the main library by 5 p.m., so we hurried along and completed our work. By the end of the day, I estimated that we had issued some 600 books, and it had not been a busy day at that, so I was well pleased with my efforts. Mrs. Burch asked me if I had enjoyed myself.

'Yes indeed,' I replied in answer to her kind enquiry, 'I'm sure I shall enjoy every minute of it.'

Mind you, in the depths of winter, when our fingers froze to the book cards, and the van slipped and skidded on the treacherous ice, I sometimes wondered about the accuracy of my prediction, but on the whole, I can say most sincerely that I had been right.

For the rest of that week, I was kept busy serving books to my readers and attending to their requests. What a variety of places we visited too, ranging from the humble white-washed cottages of the elderly people, to neat, newly built housing estates inhabited mostly by young married couples, to a few very large and well maintained detached residences – obviously the homes of the local 'gentry'. The number of farms that we visited was absolutely terrific – I'm sure we must have gone to forty, even in that first week. We also called at local village halls and shops, which were the focal point for our readers to gather and await our arrival, whilst exchanging gossip.

Daily we frequented the local inns and pubs (not because we were alcoholics but because many licensees wanted our services and again, the local pub was a natural focal point for village gatherings), where there was often much hilarity.

On the Friday, it rained steadily all day and I was amused to see my readers marching up to the van, clad in over-sized gumboots and long mackintoshes right down to their ankles. Many of the older women in one village we visited wore an old straw hat as well, and I wondered what effect if any this would have in keeping off the rain. I was soon to find out!

Mrs Frobisher bounced into the van, shook herself like a dog, and leaned over my table to retrieve her books from her shopping bag. A small torrent of water gushed from the brim of her ancient straw hat, and, with alarming accuracy, poured itself down inside the collar of Bill's jacket as he sat with his back against the table. Bill looked up, startled.

'What's that?' he exclaimed, as the cold water penetrated his woolly vest!

'Oh I'm so sorry,' exclaimed Mrs Frobisher, blushing profusely and flinging her tattered hat into her bag. 'My hat keeps off the rain very well, but all the water collects in the brim and it's a nuisance trying to remember to get rid of it.'

Bill was not amused and grumpily acknowledged her apology with a surly smile. However, to make amends, Mrs Frobisher brought us out two steaming cups of Bovril and homemade biscuits which I, at any rate, enjoyed very much.

That day was rather miserable as we had to cope not only with a large number of dripping readers, but also with all their equally wet paraphernalia, such as umbrellas, macs, polythene, rain-mates and soggy plastic bags into which they deposited their books. We managed very well though, really, and were rewarded with an issue of some 800 books – not bad for such a nasty day!

Halcombe Village

Chapter Two

Autumn

AUTUMN had arrived, and that first week was the predecessor of many more to come and, as day followed day, I became more and more interested in my work and equally interested in the warmhearted, friendly and stimulating people whom I encountered. Many of my readers were middle-aged or pensioners, but we had a certain proportion of young wives and mothers who attended regularly, and I was interested to see their choice in reading. We also encountered many unusual and individual characters, who afforded me great pleasure and sometimes amusement!

One Tuesday, I think it was, we were speeding towards our destination, a small village way out on the moors, when we were surprised to see by the roadside in front of us a small figure in uniform waving madly. Apparently it was the local postmistress who, cycling between villages on her round, had fallen off the cycle and twisted her ankle. Bill and I got her and the cycle inside the van, and took her to the village for treatment. She was worried, however, about the mail which needed to be delivered in the village which we were visiting. Suddenly I had an idea!

'Have you much mail, Mrs Lyle?' I asked.

'No, only about twenty letters this morning,' she replied.

'Well, if any of these are our readers we can give them the letters when they come for books, and take the neighbours' too,' I suggested.

Mrs Lyle agreed happily, and we sorted the letters according to our reader's names. I realised, not for the first time, that we were not only expected to provide a library service to the country people, but to share in their way of life as well. This meant being as helpful as possible, and we frequently exchanged messages, delivered items of news, papers and parcels etc., to our regular customers.

The villagers expressed concern at Mrs Lyle's ankle and readily agreed to take neighbours' letters, where necessary. After depositing Mrs Lyle at the local doctor's we went on our way. What a lovely day it was too, with the pellucid blue sky above bleak rolling moors which for me at any rate held a beauty of their own. The bracken, now a lovely caramel colour, stretched for miles, interspersed with sparkling streams which rushed gaily down the hillsides, and not for the first time did I bless my job, which allowed me to see all this natural beauty.

Already, the last few swallows were perched on the telegraph wires, or circled above, ready to leave us for another year and their long flight abroad. I am a keen nature lover, and these sights inspired and elated me. Our next stop was at 'Crows Nest Lane,' and as we approached I remembered that we had a very awkward reader (one of few I hasten to add) to deal with. A more garrulous person I have yet to meet. She persisted in entering the van, and after choosing her books, would spend half an hour telling you why she had chosen this or that or any other irrelevant subject she could think of. On this particular day she was more trying than usual, and in a polite but firm effort to interrupt her chit-chat, I dropped a pile of books onto her foot. She was much too thick skinned to take offence and spent a quarter of an hour telling me about an operation she'd had on her little toe! I suppose it served me right really, and I resolved in future to grin and bear it, even though it made us late on our subsequent stops.

As we travelled over the moors between villages on the Belmont Road, I noticed the phalanx of fir trees planted by the local water boards to prevent soil erosion and beautify their reservoirs. They, together with the mountain ash trees, which bore magnificent bunches of scarlet berries, made a lovely autumn scene. Few people realise how much picturesque scenery Lancashire has to offer, just a few miles from those famous 'dark satanic mills'.

Before the next village, we had a new stop to make. A lady by the name of Mrs Emma Crow had telephoned our H.Q. and asked could we supply her with books, as she was some distance away from our other stopping places. Always eager for new custom we fitted her into the rota, and I decided to call and announce our arrival, as she did not yet know our method of blowing the horn. True to our promise, we stopped at her gate and I knocked on the door, delighted to initiate her into the joys of reading.

I rapped sharply, and the door opened quickly to reveal a small lugubrious looking woman with pale watery eyes and thinning hair.

'Oh, it's the library is it?' she said, noting the van outside.

I was just going to invite her into the van when I was interrupted by loud yappings, which continued with increasing velocity. Mrs Crow turned, and gave vent in a voice that belied her delicate looks:

'Stella stop that B . . . yapping!'

I stepped back a few paces to escape a further blast from her throat, and suddenly a large greasy-looking Dachshund appeared, followed by another, and another, then several smaller ones, until they were all milling round my feet and legs.

'The gate!' shrieked Mrs Crow. 'Close the gate or they'll be in the van!'

I hurried forward, or rather tried to hurry, as I was constantly tripped and hampered by the Dachshunds, who must have had a passion for books and presumably knew how to read, for they all swarmed up the steps and into the van before I could stop them.

Bill looked round in amazement as he was soon surrounded by sticky paws and wet noses all over his cab. Mrs Emma Crow bounded inside.

'Out!' she yelled. 'Home girls, home!' she ordered, as if directing a girls' school class.

Funnily enough, the dogs seemed to recognise defeat and, led by Stella, they all trouped out and marched up the path to the tune of 'Colonel Bogey' which Mrs Crow whistled.

'I'm so sorry,' she said, 'Do excuse them, it won't happen again.'

'It was my fault for leaving the gate open,' I answered, and hastened to arouse her literary interest with our books. After this incident,

Mrs Lillian Hutchings of The Gate House, Belmont Road, one of our best customers

however, she became one of our best-loved readers, and I eagerly looked forward to seeing her, and the dogs, which I later discovered she bred.

And so time sped by, my life ebbing away with it. Not all the days were fine, it's true. But that year we were blessed with a particularly clear, crisp, golden October and there was just enough nip of cold to make the nostrils tingle when you breathed in the fresh country air.

I revelled in the autumn sun, now pale as it struggled across the rugged slopes of the Darwen Moors. As the days grew shorter, I watched the leaves turn from amber and orange, first to crimson then to brown, until finally they cascaded about us in whirling eddies as we cruised down the country lanes.

Another village which we visited was particularly renowned for its beauty. Sure enough, as we pulled up next to the village green, a charming sight met our eyes. Set around the green itself were masses of horse chestnuts, now a lovely flame colour. The neat little white- or cream-washed cottages were surrounded by gardens offering a glorious array of dahlias and michaelmas daisies. The village green was of particular interest to me, as it sported not only the renowned duck-pond, but a real pair of village stocks, which, as I had been informed furtively by one of the residents, were still used for erring youths. (I reserved my doubts as to this truth.)

We had quite a crowd of readers here and were kept well occupied for a good half hour. After our work we were treated to afternoon tea, though Mrs Thoms' idea of tea was two pieces of dried oatcakes and a cup of tea so weak you could literally read through it. (Bill called it shamrock tea – meaning three leaves.) Mrs Thoms herself was a small, nervous woman, with beady eyes like blackcurrants and, as she always stayed in the van and talked to us, we were forced to eat the oatcakes, which I'm sure were flavoured with sawdust.

'Is the tea alright, dear?' she would ask.

'Oh fine' I answered her, choking over the dry oatcake, and hoping my face hid the truth. However, we were thankful for small mercies, and, in winter especially, the tea, although so weak, was very welcome.

The last stop in Turton was at a lovely old farm, owned by a Mr and Mrs O'Shea, a lively but rather eccentric couple who, in addition to the usual farm livestock kept bees, goats and a large flock of swans on a stretch of river. These animals and birds were treated as members of the family and wandered in and out of the farmhouse ad-lib (I'm sorry to say), causing their owner chaos.

After Mrs O'Shea had chosen her books, we prepared to leave and Bill drove down the farm track, when suddenly in front of us, right in our path, we saw a fat Mallard duck. Bill stopped and blew the horn, but no matter, the bird sat stubbornly and refused to move. I was stepping out to shoo her away, when Mrs O'Shea rushed up, waving her arms and shrieking.

'Don't move her, she's broody, and I don't want her upsetting!'

'Brooding!' I cried, misinterpreting the word, 'But it's the wrong time of the year surely?'

Mrs O'Shea explained, 'I mean she's in one of her broody moods, and she musn't be moved or she may take offence. She's my favourite you know, and very delicate.'

I was rather taken aback by this information!

'Surely you don't mean we must wait until she decides to move herself?' I said. 'We have to get back to H.Q.'

'You can't go till she goes.' said Mrs O'Shea firmly.

Bill had by now joined us, and was listening to the conversation with some amusement.

'Well we can't go round her,' he said, 'so I'll just have to go over her, and if she doesn't move we'll have roast duck tomorrow.'

Mrs O'Shea's face was a bright crimson and, with a shriek, she made a grab at the offending duck, who gave a loud squawk and flapped off into the trees, with Mrs O'Shea hot on her heels. With no time to lose, we rushed into the van and drove off, trying to ignore the loud and rude comments which came from the trees. So much for another eventful day, I mused, as we headed back to the library.

St Anne's Church, Turton

Chapter Three

The W.I.

NOVEMBER sauntered in, cold, wet, miserable and gloomy. We meandered round country lanes, watching the hedgerows with their stark branches dripping rivulets of murky rain into the sluggish ditch below, and bedraggled robins and blue tits taking shelter.

Everyone's comments were about the weather. Most of our readers in the more remote places became noticeably depressed as day followed damp day. Bill and I did our best to cheer them up, but we both caught severe colds and were in no mood to tolerate the little fads of individual readers. In fact, it was during this particular period that I lost my temper with a customer (the one and only time I did, by the way).

A number of our readers were notorious for retaining books for long periods if they possibly could. But because these books were often requested by other people (they were usually the more popular type in constant demand), I felt it necessary to press for them to be returned regularly each visit. Some of the readers (dear old souls) had different ideas, however; they hoarded books like gold and guarded them jealously if I asked for their return.

One such person was Tommy Riley, a dirty old recluse who always wore the same clothes – ragged black trousers, caked with mud, shabby tweed jacket, and a red and black Tam o' Shanter with what should have been a red, but which was now a pure black, bob on top. I'll swear he'd never heard of soap, as his complexion was the colour of smoked haddock and his matted hair poked out in wisps from under the Tam o' Shanter.

He drove an equally dirty Landrover round the villages, and if he missed us calling at his home because he was out in the fields, when he saw the van he would 'view – halloo' us from the distance and make a wild dash across the lanes towards us. He also had a nasty habit of suddenly pulling out of side lanes, taking off his Tam o' Shanter and flagging us down.

When he did enter the van and eventually produced the books from the vast depths of a huge Gladstone bag, he'd either forgotten to bring half of them back, or I would find charming bookmarks inside, such as a kipper bone or, once, a dried frog's leg. I really got annoyed about this, and one dreary November day, which had been particularly trying, we were just setting off for H.Q. when Farmer Riley careered carelessly round a corner, and screeched to a halt right in front of us so that Bill was forced to stop. When he entered the van and slapped down the books and two field mice, who had evidently decided to hibernate in his bag, jumped out and raced gaily round the shelves, that did it! To put it bluntly I told the farmer he was a nuisance, a pest, an irresponsible twit who wasn't fit to borrow books which belonged to the public, and if he didn't mend his ways, I would suspend his membership.

As I ranted on his face grew longer, and he looked like a little boy standing there, so I started to feel sorry and calmed down a little. He explained that his wife had died twenty years ago and he'd so much to think about, he just couldn't remember to look after the books or bring them all back, let alone catch us at the right time and place. Well, he looked so pathetic that I felt ashamed of my outburst, and his moving saga of how his only pleasure was 'book at bedtime' nearly had me in tears, so I relented and let him off if he promised to try and do better. He did for almost four weeks, by which time he was back again at his usual antics, so I just decided to turn a blind eye. Bill later told me that many others before me had tried to reform him, but no one had yet succeeded.

It appeared that most of the villages we visited had established branches of the Women's Institute, and very popular they seemed to be, too, especially in winter.

In one village in particular I noted that it seemed to flourish extremely well, and as W.I. night was Tuesday and we visited the village the day after, our library became the focal point for exchanging views and comments on the previous night's activities and often criticisms of the unfortunate speakers.

The Marsh Lane branch of the W.I. was also renowned for its trips and outings, details of which were recounted to us with great gusto by grateful members. One Wednesday, we arrived as usual to find only half our usual number of readers at the main stop. 'Where is everybody?' I asked. 'Is there a flu epidemic?' (This last remark was prompted by the spell of unusually cold and damp weather which we had experienced during late November.)

'Oh no,' someone informed me, 'it's the W.I.'s luncheon party today; they've all been to the Spread Eagle in Preston but they'll be back soon.'

Someone else added, 'They've not forgotten it's your day.'

Sure enough, fifteen minutes later, a coach drew up, and we saw our missing readers, who called to us to wait for them whilst they collected their books. The luncheon party must have gone down well, as all our customers seemed very merry and bright, a few even giving forth polite belches behind discreet hands. I asked quite a few if they had enjoyed themselves, and when they belched politely I indicated that Andrews or Alka-Selzter was a good stomach settler, or produced a book on medicine.

We were interrupted in the middle of all this by the boisterous

A group of readers make their choice

arrival of two elderly, widowed and rather narrow-minded sisters, who evidently only emerged from their cottage at Christmas and other special occasions. They mounted the van steps with some difficulty and I was greatly amused by the way they waved their arms and walking sticks in an effort to keep upright. As I knew that they were of a mild and innocent temperament, I couldn't resist poking a little fun at them.

'Have you enjoyed yourself then?' I asked the elder.

'Yes indeed,' she replied, balancing her books gaily on her swaying hip. The younger, Elsie, was not quite so cheerful now. In fact she looked rather green, but Doris, the elder, was positively bubbling over with delight.

'I've had a Shandy and a Cherry Brandy and a Lager and a . . .'

This would have gone on for ever if Elsie had not interrupted by falling against Doris and knocking all her books flying.

'Dear me!' I exclaimed, 'are you quite well? I do declare, Mrs Barnes, you've been on the beer again. Shall I ask Mrs Ronson [the local nurse] to chaperone you?'

This last remark of mine was greeted by a shout of laughter from the other readers who were all eyes and ears to witness the drama.

Elsie Barnes, however, took offence at these remarks and said stoutly, 'I'm quite well thank you, Mrs Moore, and I've not been on the beer. In fact,' she continued, drawing herself up to her full height as best she could, 'I've tasted my first ever Martini.'

'Oh you devil, you!' said someone at the back, and I gathered from the murmurs and twinkling glances that some of the W.I. members had secretly decided to get the straight-laced sister a trifle tight. To put it bluntly they had certainly succeeded, or so it seemed, for by now Doris was careering round the van with a huge pile of books which included Tennessee Williams and John Braine (not I may hasten to add her usual type.)

The W.I. members joined in the fun and began to tease Elsie again.

'Shall I help you dear?' said one.

'You really should lie down, Elsie, I'm surprised at you,' said another.

'Fancy coming drunk to the Library. You're a sly one,' said another.

'Fancy pretending to be teetotal.'

Poor Elsie wasn't enjoying this at all, and vainly tried to dismiss her teasers. By now she was dull and grey, so I offered her my stool to sit on.

'Oh no really I couldn't,' she protested; 'I do feel rather full though.'

I pushed the stool towards her and she sat down, resting her back against my table. She seemed quite settled, so I again turned my attention to the other readers who were looking on with amusement as Doris with both arms full of books tottered towards the door.

'Just a minute, let me take out the tickets please,' I said.

But Doris couldn't wait and before I could grab hold of her, she tripped on the top step and the books flew out all over the road in all directions, followed swiftly by Doris herself. W.I. members hastily rushed to rescue both from their predicament. Luckily Doris had landed on the grass verge and was only shaken, but it was decided by the members to escort both of the sisters home and see them to bed. Elsie meanwhile, left unattended during this little drama, had slipped sideways across my table and was snoring peacefully. She was carried off by laughing W.I. members who said it had been one of the jolliest Christmas lunches ever.

The day wore on, brightened by our incident. We wound our way down a narrow country lane so beset with potholes and boulders that I thought we would be flung into the ditch at any moment. It's a tribute to Bill's driving that I am alive to write this tale. A slight sprinkling of snow over a heavy frost made the track even more treacherous and I wondered, not for the first time, was our journey really necessary? It was like being on safari as the van bumped its way up the lane.

Our first port of call was at a small 'one up, one down' cottage, inhabited by Mrs Maggie Brunshaw. She was a dear, really, but very deaf and she had a great fear of being run over by our van. As Bill blew the horn, she opened the door and shouted.

'Just a minute whilst I get round, don't move until I get in.'

Then, she mounted the steps, puffing slightly and gasped, 'I'm always feared of you setting off before I get here.'

As she said this every time I had to stop myself from retorting sharply – not that I got much chance to retort anything, as Mrs Brunshaw shouted everything on account of her being deaf, and my answers to her went unnoticed.

'Are you going anywhere at Christmas, Mrs Brunshaw?' I shouted.

She paused, looked up from the bookshelves and retorted, 'No thanks, I'd rather have a romance.'

I tried again. 'I asked you about Christmas.'

'Oh,' she exclaimed, the penny dropping (or so I thought) 'my sister – yes, she will, thanks.'

I gave up and retired into the latest Georgette Heyer whilst she chose her books.

As she went out, she made her inevitable last remark, 'Don't set off until I get round you.' I smiled tolerantly and shut the door after her with a sigh.

Our last stop of the day was at a picturesque old farm at the top of the lane. We arrived on time without mishap, and Bill reversed neatly (or so he thought) into the farmyard. Suddenly, there was a terrific clatter coming from the rear, and Bill tried to draw forward, but the van simply wouldn't move – we appeared to be stuck! I jumped out to see what had happened. It appeared that Bill had misjudged his reverse and, instead of doing a neat turn, had bumped into the henhouse stocked ready for the spring. What a commotion! The unfortunate hens flew all over the place – in the van, on the roof, on my shoulders, shrieking and squawking in sheer terror. They scattered about the yard like snowflakes in the wind, running between my legs, as I vainly tried to estimate the damage. It appeared that we had demolished one side of the wooden hen hut completely and, judging by the noise they made, I expect those hens didn't settle or lay for some weeks afterwards. The stentorion voice of the farmer suddenly brought us to our senses, as I vainly tried to pluck hen feathers and hen dirt from my clothes and hair.

It was unfortunate for us that he was one of our most awkward customers, as a more obdurate old man I've yet to meet. Bill was woebegone.

'What the hell is he going to say?' he murmured to me as the farmer stood, rugged, hands on brawny hips, staring at the fleeing hens. I

The unfortunate hens flew all over the place!

decided to leave Bill to explain as it was his driving which had caused the accident, and I attempted to pursue the shrieking hens, who were by now out of the farmyard and careering wildly down the lane – not an easy task I assure you. I was soon joined by the farmer's daughter, who fortunately (unlike her father) had a sense of humour and saw the whole thing as a great joke. Those hens would not be caught. Either it was the cold weather which made them more lively, or they were frightened by the sight of me, but whichever it was we must have looked funny, chasing down the lane, snatching at Rhode Island Reds and White Leghorns who ignored our pleas to 'hush now' and turned and pecked us viciously.

Eventually, however, we rounded up the marauding hens (except for a few which continued to flap wildly over hill and dale, and are still on the run to this day, I expect) I returned to the scene of the crime to see what Mr Robson had said. As I feared, the worst had happened. He was very annoyed, said we would have to pay for the damage and that he didn't want any more books from us. I tried to soothe him, but to no avail, so I made out the necessary insurance forms before we left. Bill was upset, poor chap. I felt sorry for him – anybody can have an accident.

Inside the van was complete chaos as hens had flapped in and out continuously since I had chased the others and they all seemed to have left their 'calling cards' (obviously in lieu of a library ticket!). Feathers floated and fluttered everywhere and a few of the cheekier ones were still in the cab pecking at my tea. I chased them out, swept out the van and then turned my attention to myself. What a sight I must have looked! Trews covered in mud stains and hen manure, and feathers stuck all over my face. I decided to wash properly at the Library, as farmer Robson was obviously anxious for us to depart, and so, thankfully, we escaped from his wrath.

However, things didn't turn out quite so badly, as Mrs Robson managed to pour oil on troubled waters and when the hen house had been repaired, we were asked to resume our library service once more.

Chapter Four

Visit of the Mobile Library
to 'Clogstown'

IT WAS a cold, damp rather misty November morning, when the
driver and myself set off over the moors to the small village of
'Clogstown' (about four miles east of Blackburn). We had been
asked to organise a new library service there, by making monthly
visits to as many places as possible. We knew the place was rather
remote, but as we approached a small cluster of buildings from the
moors, my heart sank – what hopes were there here, in a place as
sparse as this, of providing some useful literature? Fortunately, as we
got nearer, I could see that the buildings were, in fact, henhouses (my
mistake). Even so we were totally unprepared for the sight which met
our eyes.

'Clogstown' consisted, in actual fact, of about 100 houses, neatly
arranged on each side of the narrow bumpy road, plus a few cottages
perched on the top of what must have been a very windy hill. Why
'town', I mused, hamlet or village would be more like it? But I was
wrong again, for at least ten people lived in each two up and two down
house (or so it seemed). As our red van appeared at the top of the main
street a 'view-halloo' sounded throughout the place. Doors opened,
clogs clattered, dogs barked, bearded old men cleaned their spectacles
and mob-capped women stopped their scrubbing to stare at us.
Nothing like it had ever appeared before apparently. There were
shouts in deep Lancashire accents of 'whods thad?', 'sitha Joe yon red
thing up theer is it one o yon mizzles [missiles] er summat?'

Delighted – yet amazed – at the excitement we had caused, I opened
the door wider to hear more of the amazing comments. We had by now
stopped at the row of 'Windy Cottages' and in two minutes were
surrounded by curious spectators of all ages; cloth-capped old men
with their sticks, two middle-aged women with their hair in curlers and
the typical Lancashire overall, were crowding round us, carefully
examining the van both inside and out.

One very short-sighted woman looking at the shelves said, 'Where's the sugar and t'butter? It's not as good as Co-op van is it? Is there any divvy?'

Her daughter tried to explain. 'It's nod Co-op ma, its Library with some books fer us.'

The look on the old woman's face made me choke with laughter.

'Libry' she said: 'Whads that doin' here. Have we nod paid enough fer this wi 'Red Letter' an 'Woman' costin 8d?'

'No, no, ma,' insisted her daughter, 'these are free, owt o't rates for us.'

'Free are they, o well thads diffrent then' said the old woman; then turning to me she stated: 'I'll have two luv tales, miss, with plenty of thad theer in.'

At that critical moment I was trying to make myself heard above the bedlam.

'Will you all please give me your names and addresses, then choose your books,' I shouted, but the old woman persisted.

'I said two luv tales an quick about it!' she yelled.

I decided to oblige, gave her two love tales and pushed her towards the door. No use telling her to look around the shelves, I thought, nor indeed was it any use telling anyone. They were all so bewildered and were under my feet like sheep, before any sort of order was formed.

Eventually we got their names and addresses and to a great muttering of 'ohs' and 'ahs' and 'sitha theer Bill yons a book about t'flowers,' we managed to do some work.

If I thought the first stop was busy, it wasn't a patch on stop two. As we coasted down the main street and stopped at the bottom of the hill, a crowd rolled up. Apparently an argument was going on. A huge man of about eighty stood banging his stick on the cobbles. As I opened the door he said: 'I tell thee I'm t'chairman 'ere, and I'm fost in so tha knows,' and he gave a smart kick with his clogs at the crowd to reinforce his statement.

Rather taken aback I said smartly, 'Yes Sir, can I help you, what sort of books do you like?'

To my amazement he pointed his stick at me and glaring said: 'I want no lip from thee lass, I can choose whad I like when I like.'

Another awkward customer I thought, how many more were there like this?

Suddenly, pressure from outside swept the chairman to the back of the van and out of my sight – thank goodness. For the next hour, I was deluged with comments, requests, exclamations and all kinds of weird remarks, which I had to translate as best I could.

Everyone spoke in dialect, which I often found hard to understand. On asking one elderly lady her address she replied: 'Top o' t' sugar field.'

'Pardon?' I said as politely as I could. 'Where?'

'Tha num bugger, I mean up theer,' she said pointing vaguely in the direction of the sun. Some kind person eventually explained that the old lady's address was actually 'Sweet Loves Lane' commonly known as Top o' t' sugar field.

This was only one of the quaint addresses we had; some of the gems were 'Honey Hole', 'Pudding Nook', (after a woman who died of eating black puddings), 'T'Glory Hole', 'Mucky Dick's Lane', and many other enchanting places.

The villagers' knowledge of literature was very limited, I'm afraid. One dear old man, peering through his spectacles, made one request which completely threw me.

'Hast tha any o' Charlies luv?'

I replied trying to think of an author called Charles,

'Aye, tha knows, Charly Dickens, thowd old dodger an all that,' he explained.

Of course, he meant Charles Dickens. Another sweet old thing asked for a book by one 'Dorothy Swan' – apparently written in the year dot.

How long had it been since anyone from the twentieth Century had been here, I wondered? There seemed to be a lack of youngsters, even accounting for the ones at school, and we usually got lots of children on our other visits. The population were uniformly alike, I observed. The men (not one under 65) all wore checked cloth caps, trousers three sizes too big for them, dark navy waist coats and an old pin-striped jacket plus, of course, the clogs for which their village was famous. The women (all over 50) wore either hairnets or curlers, navy spotted overalls were sported by the younger ones of 60-70, whilst the others had shawls and long dusty skirts.

Most of the population also appeared to be deaf (perhaps something to do with the high altitude, I thought!).

On that first visit, I returned home sounding hoarse after shouting for three hours to answer their cries. This deafness also led to some amusing mistakes on the villagers' parts, as I found out on future visits. One old man stunned me completely one day when in answer to my question, 'What would you like?' he shouted to me:

'Why tha cheeky young madam, thee go an get someone tha own age.' He thought I'd said 'what are you doing tonight?" Such was life, and on each visit I grew more and more intrigued by the inhabitants of 'Clogstown'.

They were certainly appreciative of the service if nothing else. Each visit we were greeted warmly by a huge queue with bags and baskets full of books, each clamouring to be first in 'T Libry' as it became known. Their appreciation was very sincere; one day a very deaf old man grasped my hand and said in terribly loud voice: 'Thank you for these treasures – books are wonderful, real treasures.' He really meant it, and I felt very touched by his obvious sincerity, even though everyone in the van at the time had stopped to witness the little episode.

We got more strange and obscure requests, and it needed an enormous amount of time and patience to sort them out. We were asked for '10 Black Bottoms' which turned out to be *Ten Little Niggers*, 'Tum cat wi t'hot foot' (*Cat on a hot tin roof*), and 'Far from t'rumpus' (*Far from the Madding Crowd*) to name but a few. These and many others appeared with amazing regularity and it seemed to be that when one person discovered a 'treasure' the whole village read it.

Despite all these trials and tribulations I became very fond of the villagers, and I believe they of me too. As we got to know each other better, I was offered cups of tea, cake, plants, biscuits (once even a bottle of rum at Christmas). At each visit a woman would secretly deposit a bag of jelly babies on to my seat and I had to thank her in muttered tones, as it would be sacrilege to let Emma find out.

Emma was the village humbug, a wizened old lady who terrified the whole community, and I was no exception. She would enter the van and the conversation would halt abruptly. Everyone would make way for her to have her books checked in. Everyone else in the village called me 'T'little lass' (notwithstanding the fact that I was a married woman of 27) but not so Emma. She would eye me coldly and say, 'Two detectives with plenty of blood and thunder.' I usually obliged her to get her out quickly, but one day I was a little slower than usual and she delivered her 'blessing' to me. As she was still shouting she tripped on the top step and fell headfirst on the pavement. She never came near the library again, much to everyone's relief.

Everyone seemed very friendly – like one big happy family in the village, and they frequently used the library day to exchange the usual gossip.

One gem of a conversation was carried on in my presence whilst I was checking the books:

'Hasta sin yon theer in Marks and Sparks, Lizzie?'

'Whads thad?' said Lizzie.

'Tha knows,' said Ada. 'one o them new fangled strings to keep thi stockins up'.

'I dorn't need owt like that,' replied Lizzie; 'I 'as some garters left by me Grannie 50 years ago an ther still good yet.'

In such cases as this, it was very difficult for me not to laugh, so I usually started eating the jelly babies to divert attention.

"I 'as some garters left by me Grannie 50 years ago and ther still good yet!"

Each visit one lady descended on us with a huge black bag containing only 6 books, and requested 'Six novels fer Aunty Tilly please, as she wouldn't come herself.' I wondered who was Aunty Tilly, visualising a dear old bedridden lady. But no – one day 'Aunty Tilly' materialised and what a surprise! She turned out to be a spruce but eccentric maiden lady of 55-60 years with huge high heels and a large black cloak round her shoulders which gave her the appearance of a bat. I was enchanted. As last this mysterious woman was here, but as she wore a deaf aid and shouted like the rest of the villagers she soon lost some of her charm of the unknown.

One day, near Christmas time, an old gent came in and gave me a parcel. 'That's for thee and him,' he said pointing at Bill. A strong aroma came from the parcel, and on opening it two big black puddings fell out. Bill and I looked at each other and as soon as we left the village, out they went, but the smell lingered for weeks.

The post office at Belthorn Village, the focal point for many of our readers

Mrs Molly Woods of Chapeltown Road, Turton, bringing coffee for Mrs Moore and driver, as she did for many years

Hob Lane which leads down to Wayoh Reservoir

Mary Alice Berry of Belthorn eagerly awaits the arrival of the mobile library

90-year-old Mrs Nancy Gabbatt outside her home in Bethorn receives her books from Mrs Moore

Harry Jolley fishes at Entwistle Reservoir

Chapter Five

The Blizzard

A COLD nip was in the air – I donned an extra sweater and bought myself a crocheted hat ready to face the perils of the countryside in winter. I decided warmth came before books. Early one mid-December morning we set off on our fortnightly visit to the village of Withnell. As it would be our last visit before Christmas to many places I decided to take extra stock so that readers could have more books during the holidays if they wished.

Our first port of call before reaching the village was at a lonely farm high up above the road, commanding a magnificent view of the surrounding moors. The slight falling of snow some days before had almost gone. The ground was clear, though slippy, so we were able to travel as usual. I gazed with pleasure at the stark branches of trees, pushing their way upwards towards the sky, as if in defiance of winter. A few friendly robins hopped by us over the walls on the back side of the track, and the sheep could still be seen in their warm woolly coats nuzzling for grass in the hard ground.

High Ridge Farm was owned by a Mrs Thomas, a rather eccentric but sweet person, and a lover of dogs, and indeed animals of all kinds. She had about twenty dogs of all different breeds, shapes and sizes and she exhibited most of them at local shows etc.. On this particular morning, we were greeted by loud barks and yappings as we drew into the yard. Mrs Thomas climbed into the van and began to discuss books with me, but we were constantly interrupted by loud yappings and sorties made at the van door. Mrs Thomas looked out into the yard to see what the matter was and, as my gaze followed hers, I nearly fell out of the van with laughing. At her porch, tied with a long rope, were four massive Bull Terriers, who bore the classic names of Annabelle, Jezebel, Gertrude and Penelope. I had seen them before, but not like this, for each one sported a brightly coloured jumper – its front paws thrust into the sleeves, and its head through a narrow gap finished off by neatly fastened pearl buttons back and front. Each jumper had a basic main colour, but had horizontal strips of a contrasting hue, which made the poor animals look more incongruous and prodigious than ever.

Mrs Thomas must have seen my reaction
'Oh, don't you think it's a good idea to keep them warm this weather?' she expounded, 'I should hate them to catch a cold – after all you've got an extra jumper on haven't you?' she said, noting my red sweater and bulging figure.

'Yes, but I hope I don't look like that,' I thought as I hastily agreed how sensible she was.

Each one sported a brightly coloured jumper

The dogs stopped yapping as soon as Mrs. Thomas spoke tenderly to them, 'I'm coming darlings – just a moment, Mummy won't be long.' I wondered, not for the first time, why Mrs Thomas had had no children; her copious affections were clearly wasted on these noisy and highly belligerent animals. They were still causing me to laugh as they pulled and strained at their ropes, looking rather like runners waiting for the gun. However, I managed to control my face twitchings and attended to my duties.

We left Mrs Thomas and bumped down the hill. I gazed at the winter stream, meandering sluggishly by the roadside. Sparrows twittered noisily, hoping for tit-bits and little sparkles of frost twinkled at us from the hedges. Our next call, just outside the village, was at a small detached house called Hawthorne Cottage just by the roadside. It was inhabited by two middle-aged spinster sisters; the Misses Scarlett and Opal Sandys.

As we drew into the side and blew the horn, I wondered (not for the first time) why the elder had been given the name Scarlett. Had her mother been reading *Gone with the Wind* when she gave birth, I mused? But this morning as I glanced round, the answer became clear, or so it seemed to me at any rate. There on the line, flapping gaily in the gentle breeze, and with legs frozen solid, were several pairs of scarlet bloomers each with legs long enough to cover a Giraffe, let alone the diminutive Miss Scarlet!

'My word, there's more in these two than meets the eye!'

Bill, following my gaze, burst out laughing. We were interrupted in our mirth by the appearance of Miss Scarlett herself, with two steaming cups of coffee and a plate of homemade cookies.

'I think it's really chilly this morning,' she ventured, 'so I thought you could do with this to help you on your way.'

'How nice of you,' I said, and immediately felt ashamed at my recent mocking.

However, she was not to know, and whilst we drank the coffee she twittered on gaily about her plans for Christmas and the presents she had made. I asked after her sister Miss Opal, who when she came to the van always looked absolutely worn-out and defeated, her thin face creasing with worried lines.

'Oh she's out this morning, gone Christmas shopping on her bike,' ventured Miss Scarlett.

'I hope she watches the roads then,' I said, 'it's rather slippy.'

'Oh, Opal can look after herself, never fear, she'll be back after dinner, in fact you may see her on your rounds.'

(I made a mental note to look out for two thin legs encased in green tights trundling the cycle along the country lanes.) After saying this, Miss Scarlett twitched towards the door with her pile of books, wished us a Merry Christmas and departed, back to the warmth of her bloomers (once she'd thawed the legs out).

Dead on time, we arrived in Withnell and were soon surrounded by our usual crowd of enthusiastic readers, full of talk and chatter about local Christmas events. There was the usual bazaar and Christmas Fayre, which this year I understood boasted a tombola and a bingo session (highly unusual in the Methodist Church). I listened to the gossip with interest and amusement. Dear readers, so content in their own country way, demanding so little of life. How nice, I thought, to get away from the fast moving, high tension living of the big towns, and be able to relax and enjoy the simple amenities life has to offer in the country.

As the day wore on it became raw and gloomy, and the once blue sky turned a dark shade of grey.

'Looks like snow's on the way,' murmured Bill; 'not fall for a day or two yet though – until it gets warmer,' he added. We were now well out on the moors above Belmont, high above sea level, and the grey clouds loomed ominously above us, blocking our view and causing the sheep to bestir themselves and lunge slowly homewards – some instict warning them of the gathering storm. However, as Bill had predicted, no snow fell during the afternoon, and we were able to complete our rounds in comfort.

The last call of the day was at a neat row of small terraced houses just off the main track, inhabited by a wide variety of personages, ranging from the local nurse, a college student who couldn't afford anywhere else, Mrs Barnett, a lively 80 year old, and a warmhearted immigrant from Ireland, Mrs. Dooley. She was my favourite at this stop, I must confess. With hair like a wire pan scrub, and ebullient with Irish blarney, she swept into the van, clattered her books down, gave me a hearty hand shake and boomed:

'Sure and it's going to snow as true as I'm Irish. Keep weel wrapped up, mi dear.'

When I could get a word in edgeways I agreed with her remarks about the weather and asked her was she going back to Ireland for Christmas.

'To be sure I would if I could dear, but my old man's got gout and he won't budge, so here we'll stay.'

'What are you doing?' she asked, and went on to say: 'If I were you I'd go to Dublin for Christmas; oh there's some lovely lads there, make your hair curly they would mi dear. Do you like the arty types, there's some real ones there for you?'

I looked at her in amazement.

'But I don't need any lovely lads, I'm already married,' I replied.

Mrs Dooley's face was a picture, 'Oh, I'm sorry lovey – I didn't realize – you look so young', she added (probably as an afterthought to appease me). She squinted at me from under two bushy grey eyebrows. 'Come to think of it though you do have a worried look – never mind dear, you won't live forever!'

How cheerful I thought, then said to Bill: 'Isn't it time we were off?'

Luckily he caught my cue. We wished all a merry Christmas and, with an eye on the ominous grey sky, rushed home as quickly as possible.

Two days later the snow came! Softly and silently it descended, covering hills and hedges, towns and villages alike, gently coating the roads and lanes with a soft white mask. It was early morning and, as we set off on our route, I gazed with enchantment at the somnolent flakes as they covered still objects, hushing them with their touch and transforming dirty grey buildings into an unbelievable hue of whiteness. Bravely we turned off the main road on to a narrow track which led to Mrs Athins, a jolly old widow who lived alone, and eagerly awaited our visit each fortnight. As it had been snowing heavily since dawn, there was quite a lot of snow on the track and we had difficulty in turning. But we made it, and it was worth the effort to see Mrs Athins' face as Bill blew the horn.

'Oh there now, how nice to see you,' she expostulated: 'I didn't think you would get here today.'

'Oh we always come if we can' I said. 'Glad to bring you a bit of cheer anyway.'

She chose her books carefully, then said: 'Would you mind giving the greengrocer a message when you get to Edenfield? I'm out of potatoes and onions, and need some as soon as possible,' she said.

I promised to deliver the message, glad to be of service to her. As we left, the snow slackened a little, but a cool, rough wind began to blow, and lift the thickened flakes into whirlpools of white mist.

'Could get nasty if this wind gets stronger,' observed Bill, 'better hurry on our rounds and get back as quickly as possible.'

We had our dinner at a delightful little country café – homemade steak pie with vegetables, fruit tart and piping hot custard. Oh, it did taste good! Mrs Ginty the proprietor told us over our coffee that the wind was rising steadily and that several small lanes round about were already impassable.

'I shouldn't go to Fletchers Farm, I believe it's really deep up there – you can telephone from here if you like,' she said. I thanked her, and 'phoned one or two of our readers to ascertain the condition of the lanes up to their farms. Most people said we could manage, a few advised us not to attempt the drive, and some promised to meet us on the main road to save us the journey. As we turned up our collars and stepped outside the café an icy blast nearly blew us back in again. Snowflakes whirled and eddied about us, and a small drift was piling against the van wheels. We decided to do what visits we could, then go back to H.Q.

On the whole, we did well, and had almost finished except for two last stops. We turned off the road on to a farm track, which had been declared clear over the 'phone. However, as we proceeded along, it became evident that it was not clear now, and the snow was driving across the windscreen and piling up on each side of the lane. I wanted Bill to turn back, but it was too narrow to reverse without risk, and as there was no gate to reverse into until we reached Mrs Biltons, we were forced to carry on. Bill did not help matters by telling me I'd have to help if we got stuck, for as I looked outside, the sky was grey with snow and the wind, now at its peak, rushed flakes along like a snowstorm.

We eventually reached Mrs Bilton, who apologised profusely, saying that she'd thought the snow would stop when we had 'phoned, and she really did want some books for over Christmas. I served her as quickly as I could, rather annoyed at her misjudgement, but she was so friendly one could soon forgive her anything.

Bill managed to turn round successfully, and off we went, back up the lane. We had only gone a few yards, however, when the snow became so thickly plastered against the windscreen that the wipers couldn't move. 'Damn!' exclaimed Bill, 'This has turned into a regular blizzard – I fear we'll get stuck.' And get stuck we did in no uncertain terms. The van eventually came up against a wall of snow that it couldn't mount, and Bill and I braved the storm to try and dig a way through, but it was much too wide for that. 'You go back to Mrs Bilton's and 'phone, whilst I'll see if I can get chains on the wheels to help,' said Bill. 'I'll just reverse a bit to clear this drift,' he continued. He reversed, or rather tried to reverse, but he must have hit a ditch, for there was a noise like thunder from the back and 2,000 books jettisoned onto the floor. That was all I needed. I was cold, wet and miserable and by now very impatient. Bill looked morosely at the piles of books on the floor; 'Stupid ditch, couldn't see the banking for the snow.' He offered a feeble explanation and I made a quick decision:

'I'll go to Mrs Bilton, then pick up these books when I get back, if you'll see to the wheels Bill.'

The van door opened by giving it a vicious kick, which is what it needed during cold weather when it stuck. This relieved my tension somewhat and I jumped out, into a large drift I'm sorry to say, and struggled bravely towards the house. Mrs Bilton must have seen me coming. 'Oh do come in dear, you're wet aren't you?' This was the mildest understatement I'd ever come across, for by this time the snow was over my boots, and I'd fallen headfirst into a drift which covered the cold, wet ditch; hence, my trews were wringing and my coat sported rivulets of snow and water which trickled deftly into my boots. However, she was very kind and after I'd telephoned the library to say we were stuck, and they had promised to send help, she insisted that I strip off, and have a hot bath and a cup of steaming Ovaltine and buttered toast, which I relished. I was worried about Bill, but I needn't have bothered; he trudged up to the door a few minutes later, saying he couldn't put the chains on until the blizzard abated. He too enjoyed Mrs Bilton's hospitality, and we waited patiently for the blizzard to subside, or the vehicle maintenance unit to rescue us – whichever came first.

After about an hour, the wind died down a little, the snow slackened its monstrous pace, and Bill said he'd see to the chains and I decided to clear the mess of books inside the van. Mrs Bilton insisted on coming with us to help as best she could. I protested that it wasn't necessary, but come she did. She'd also lent us dry clothing whilst ours dried, and Bill looked like an old nanny goat in a dung-coloured sheepskin waistcoat and matching corduroy pants whilst I resembled a cross between a character from Dickens and one from Alison Uttley, in long grey pants three sizes too big and a cherry sweater full of moth holes.

Mrs Bilton elected to help me sort the books, but she had strange ideas of order, such as all Romances together, all Cowboys, all Crime books etc., instead of in alphabetic order. I tried to explain the system of non-fiction to her, but it was no use. Dewey numbers meant nothing to her and she ended up sorting books according to their coloured back, so I sighed and left her to it.

Bill, meantime, had attempted to put the chains on the wheels but pronounced it impossible and helped us sort the books until C.V.M.U.'s arrival. However, as darkness descended and they still didn't appear, we got colder and colder and decided to go back to Mrs B's for cocoa. As she opened the door, the 'phone was ringing violently. Mrs Bilton rushed to answer it. It was Mrs Burch for me. The C.V.M.U. couldn't come before dark and were leaving it until the morning – could I make my way home or at least back to the library with Bill? I said yes, I'd try, and told Bill of the C.V.M.U.'s decision.

We set off on the long track to the library, stumbling our way through the mounds of rippling snow. We had borrowed a torch from Mrs Bilton and in the dim twilight its light gleamed in mellowing abeisance over the uneven ground. At last, the road was in sight, and mercifully it was fairly clear as snow ploughs had been sent out. Bill flagged down a passing van and the driver, hearing our plight, took us to our H.Q.

What a day, I reflected, as I climbed into bed. My husband laughed, and said I should be paid danger money, but I didn't suffer any ill effects luckily!

Round Barn Cottages at Entwistle where we often stopped for coffee

Chapter Six

Ante-Natal-Fatal

CHRISTMAS came and went – a series of dances, parties and family gatherings – a time of carols, robins, Christmas bells and snow, bright holly berries, stickly mistletoe, gay paper wrapping, exciting parcels and tinsel Christmas cards exchanging friendly greetings between friends and heralding the start of a New Year.

After the blizzard, the van was reclaimed, and we had to miss two days whilst it was repaired, but resumed work after the Christmas and New Year break with a lifting of mind and spirit plus a new back end on the van.

The New Year awoke bright and startlingly clear with a flurry of sleet and deep frost. Roads were icy, driving treacherous, and for most of January, we had chains on the wheels to avoid further mishap. Our readers were not depressed by January, however; indeed the villages became virtual hives of industry, with Mothers Unions, the W.I., Townswomen's Guilds, and other united fellowships doing their best to enliven the dark winter days.

Blankets were knitted, plant pots decorated, cloths embroidered and dolls dressed with alarming rapidity, and we were honoured to see the finished results. Our readers would convey their products to the van for me to see, and handmade bags and baskets, handwoven scarves and warm woollen mittens frequently found their way into the piles of murder and romances which littered my desk, as their owners exchanged books.

All this bustling activity was of great interest to me, and I begged several members to teach me the old country crafts of basket weaving, crocheting and tatting, which they promised to do in due course. Each January morning, even though the sun sparkled faintly on occasions, there was still a thick frost everywhere, and the countryside looked lovely to me, even in this state. Houses and cottages were like dark cakes with layers of water icing on them, and spruce branches glistened in the morning light. Thrushes, made bold by hunger, frequented our van at dinner times and when we had sandwiches, they kept a gleaming eye out for stray crusts. In this kind of weather, when we couldn't have a dinner in a café, we often had hot soup in a flask, followed by sandwiches. It was this same soup which introduced us to Madamoiselle Lachaude and her cats.

One lunch time, we were sitting in a quiet little lay-by off the beaten track, eating soup and sandwiches, when we heard a pitiful mewing at the door, which was slightly ajar. On opening it, I beheld a little black cat, hardly bigger than a kitten, scratching at the ground and mewing feebly. There was no one around, and so I assumed that it was lost, and attracted by the smell of our soup, had wandered up to the van. I took it inside and gave it some beef soup and milk which it gulped appreciatively.

'Whoever can it belong to out here?' I said, as there were no houses around that we could see at any rate.

'Somebody has probably dumped it here' said Bill. 'Poor little blighter, what shall we do with him?'

I said 'We'll take him on our rounds this afternoon and see if we can find him a home; if not, maybe we can adopt him at the library,' I added hopefully, visualising Mrs Burch's reaction to this idea!

We prepared to set off after finishing our lunch, Benny (the cat) going with us. We were just moving slowly out of the lay-by when suddenly a little black figure appeared as if my magic in front of us. A diminutive old lady in a long black coat, purple felt hat, and a long walking cane rapped smartly on the door.

'Have you seen a little black kitten?' she asked, in broken English. 'I've lost him, and I've looked everywhere near my cottage, so I thought he may have strayed near the road.'

'Why yes! He's here,' I answered, bringing Benny towards her. She spoke in a rather foreign accent and I thought she was Dutch or something, but later I realised she was French.

'Thank you so much; my poor little Choo-Choo,' she muttered, cuddling the kitten to her. 'Is this the van that brings books round?' she added with interest. 'Do you think it's possible that I can have some?'

As I nodded in answer to her first question, she mounted the steps then ripped back the purple hat to reveal a pair of bright piercing eyes and a wizened rosy cheek, and, looking around, she said, 'I'm Madamoiselle Lachaude from 'Oozle Nest' down the lane just ahead, and I would be pleased to have some books.'

I looked at my timetable: 'Yes, we can fit you in. It must be about this time every fortnight, though, that we call.'

As it happened we usually went down Acre Lane, as it was called, on our way to a farm, but I'd never noticed 'Oozle Nest' before.

'What a quaint name,' I exclaimed, as we trundled up to the door.

'Ah yes, chosen for me by my dear cousin with whom I used to live.' said Madamoiselle Lachaude. 'I came from France 35 years ago, only for a holiday mind you, but somehow I've never got back again.' She grinned and exposed a row of empty gums, except for one tooth which protruded mournfully at the side.

As we drew up outside 'Oozle Nest' she thanked us once again for saving her cat.

'Can you spare a moment to see my other pets,' she begged. She seemed so lonely, poor soul, and so glad to see us that I decided to pop in for a moment. Delighted she led the way up the path and into the front room. As she opened the living room door what a sight met my eyes. Cats, cats, cats, everywhere; big ones, small ones, ginger toms, fluffy Persians, huge tabbies with wild eyes gazed at me from every nook and cranny. Lovely tortoishell ones hung from the curtains and crouched on the settee, black and white ones, even striped ones, they were all there mewing, scratching and scrabbling amongst themselves. She had so many I wondered how she'd missed the little black one – but like a shepherd knows his flock, Miss Lachaude knew her cats. Twenty-six she had, and knew them all by name and number!

'My goodness!' I exclaimed, 'what a collection – how do you manage to feed and keep track of them all?'

'Oh we survive' she told me. 'I've only these for company, I couldn't bear it without them.'

I felt rather sorry for her and promised to call again in two weeks with more books. At least we can relieve some of the loneliness, I reflected.

The day passed without further event, I'm glad to say, and as week followed week I found myself more and more involved and interested in the lives of these, my country readers. In one particular village our day to visit coincided with the local nurse holding an ante-natal clinic at the village hall. Many a mother-to-be has had a lift in the van to the clinic when the ground has been icy and slippery. Also we often met patients later who were unable to go to the clinic, and the nurse sent messages to them via us. Having a small daughter of my own I was keenly interested in the clinic and its babies, and tried to help if I could.

One day in particular, I remember, the ante-natal clinic was in full swing, and several mothers came into the van with their babies and books. As the ground was exceptionally slippery, Mrs Cox, the nurse and midwife, asked us to give Mrs Morton some tablets if she came in for her books, as she couldn't get to the clinic from her distant house and the baby was almost due.

True to our word, we drew up some time later outside Mrs Morton's and blew the horn for her to come out. Nothing happened, and after a while I began to wonder if I should go and knock on the door to see if she was alright, as she seldom missed her books. The curtains were drawn as I went up the path and rapped smartly on the door. At first I heard nothing, then a low moan caught my ears, I decided to go round the back. Sure enough the door was open and on the front room floor lay Mrs Morton obviously in the later stages of labour. I quickly hailed Bill and told him to go for Mrs Cox and he sped off at once. Mrs Morton was so glad to see me

'You are my last hope' she told me. 'I've felt funny all day, and was going to go for help [she had no 'phone, and no near neighbours] but I thought I'd be alright if you came with my tablets from the clinic but I'm afraid labour has started and it's come very quickly.'

I did what I could for her, brewing tea, helping her to bed and filling bottles to keep her warm. Then, as it was obvious she wouldn't reach hospital before the baby came, I asked her where her sheets and towels were. Secretly I was terrified of the baby coming before the nurse arrived. I'd had a child of my own, true, but I just couldn't remember anything about it. Then my mind went a complete blank and I certainly didn't feel I could act as a midwife. Mrs Morton began to moan and grip the bed. The contractions were getting stronger and quicker, and I lit the fire, heated water and prayed for help to come. But it didn't come quickly enough. I heard a yell from upstairs, and rushed up, just in time to deliver a healthy 6lb baby girl for Mrs Morton. I must have fainted then, for, when I came round, I was on the bed in the back room, smelling strongly of brandy and flinging my arms about in a wild frenzy. Mrs Cox grinned at me; 'You're a one aren't you, deliver a baby then flake out, no more ante-natal work for you, mi dear, its fatal.'

Once I'd recovered from the shock, I laughed too, but made a mental note never to get too involved with mothers-to-be again! Mrs Morton however, was very well and very grateful.

'Couldn't have managed without you,' she said. 'In fact as a token, I shall give baby your name as a second name, I've always liked it anyway.'

I felt rather flattered but was more than relieved to hear that the baby was well, and had suffered no ill effects from my unprofessional handling of the situation.

We got on our way once more. Luckily, we'd only one more stop after Mrs Morton but we were terribly late, so I hurried as best I could, though I was still feeling rather dazed. The last stop of the day was for an old recluse who lived at 'Sweet Nells' cottage off Cockle Dicks Lane, near Tockholes. Why he inhabited a cottage by this name I shall never know, for a more vinegary and perverse character I have yet to meet, with his piercing eyes, fumbling hands and a voice like thunder.

Israel Miller, it was rumoured, had inhabited the cottage since his wife had run off with the local magistrate some years before. As he was also addicted to raw onions and could be detected by their smell a mile off, I didn't really blame her.

Just to add to my trials, Mr Miller was exceptionally cantankerous, and he stormed round the van, cursing the stock and refusing all offers of help.

'What sort of trash is this?' he growled, picking up a new crime novel and flinging it back on the shelf – in the wrong place I noticed.

'What are you looking for, can I help you?'

'I want none of your help, young woman' he snapped, 'I was choosing books before you were born, so let me get on with it, but I wish you'd get some different books than this lot.'

I sighed and turned my attention to tidying the shelves for the next day. Israel Miller stomped round and eventually flung two old war stories on my desk.

'These will do for now,' he muttered. 'I've read them before, but there's nothing better.'

He gave a loud sniff, blew his onion breath upon us, and flounced through the door in a flurry of temper. I slammed the door after him and thankfully dozed in the front seat as Bill sped home.

The cold weather continued, with the ground hard as iron, and the trees clasping snowy burdens to their breasts. Small ponds and farmyard puddles were frozen over, and I liked to hear the crack of ice and the crisp crackle of frost made by the van wheels as we trundled and bumped our way down the sleepy country lanes. Village schools and cottages wreathed in snow, cheerful infants skidding and sliding their way home from school, frost sparkling like sugar icing, these were the sights that delighted my eyes as we dutifully carried out our work in and out of the district. But to me at any rate, it was not a duty, but a pleasure to serve the warm hearted and sympathetic people who frequented our van.

Chapter Seven

Spring Time

CROCUSES

Purest gold, purple and white,
Crocuses are sheer delight.
Heralds of the balmy Spring
When the air is fresh
And the young birds sing.
Bravely they thrust up through the earth;
Advocates of the new Spring's birth.
No frost or snow can halt their arrival
Strongly and surely, they pursue survival,
'Ere the winter's snow has scarce fled away
These little blossoms sweet and gay,
Brighten our gardens and gladden our hearts -
God's precious gift - a blessing apart.
Yes! Purest gold, purple and white
Crocuses are sheer delight!

A GENTLE wind blew from the hills, ubiquitous clouds floated in the pale blue sky, and fields became studded with daisies and coltsfoot flowers – spring had arrived. I greeted it with joy and showed my jubilation at its arrival by casting off my thick sweater and exchanging it for a brightly coloured shirt blouse.

Readers too appreciated spring, and acknowledged its arrival by turning out drawers and cupboard and holding massive jumble sales to dispose of their cast-offs. Frequently these articles found their way to our van; old straw hats, long woollen coats, odd wellington boots, cracked jugs, frayed shirts and grubby pairs of corsets with the bones hanging out. All these and many other objects were brought in discreet parcels to the van for my perusal.

'Could you do with these dear?' readers would ask in a quiet moment. I don't know whether or not I gave the impression of being poor, but some of the readers must have thought I was sadly underpaid judging by their generosity, I decided to treat myself to a couple of new outfits in order to dispel the general idea that seemed to be gaining strength; Mrs Moore is in need! Indeed I was rather affronted by all this well-meaning, but rather disconcerting arrival of goods, until Bill explained that the last librarian had often taken oddments and passed them on to poor people she knew really needed them. This was a good idea, true, but I had no intention of carrying on where my predecessor had left off.

Lines of lacy curtains flapped in the breeze, paint work shone, and bright pots of paint appeared decorating garden doors and fences, and truly proclaiming that spring was in full speight.

Moorland streams full to the brim with thawing frost and snow tumbled once more down the valleys, and fleecy lambs gambolled nonchalantly down the verdant slopes beside them. Our readers' spirits rose with each new day, and on each visit, a little of the grime of winter was swept away.

Our monthly visit to Archers Farm, near Belmont village was due, and accordingly we set off up the winding narrow track edged with murky ditches and spiky hedges. The track was so rough it was like going on a safari, and as we wound our way upwards, Bill blew the horn to sound the view-halloo to the other farms and cottages which housed our customers. It was our custom to go up to Archers Farm first, turn round then come back down the lane and serve all the others on the way down. The horn blowing was a herald to these readers to collect their books and look out for us on the way down.

We arrived at Archers Farm to be greeted by a very agitated Mrs A, and as I asked her what was the matter, I noticed a strong smell of manure filtering through the van.

'Its my grandson,' she exclaimed, 'little devil, he was playing in the yard and wandered into the dung heap right up over his knees. I've just had to clean him up before you came.'

I nodded sympathetically but didn't add that she would need to wash herself before it dried on her too. She climbed into the van and began to browse amongst the books. Suddenly she glanced through the door and let out a piercing shriek.

'John! Oh my God, he's done it again!'

We followed her gaze and beheld the luckless John again up to the knees in the dung heap and with both hands digging into the dirt and flinging the atrocious smelling manure in all directions.

'Come out of there at once,' thundered his grandmother and she leaped out of the van and grabbed the protesting John by the scruff of the neck.

'But Gran I left my toffees in there,' he said weakly.

Mrs Archer's face was a picture. Flaming red with beads of perspiration running down it, her eyes bulged and lips quivered. She dealt the offending John a blow to the ear and frog-marched him back to the kitchen sink. I'm afraid we saw the funny side of it.

'Poor little lad, he only wanted his sweets,' chortled Bill. I grinned and nodded, but quickly wiped the smile off my face as Mrs Archer sprang into the van with the velocity of a fighting tiger and smiting her hands together said:

'He's in the bath with a bottle of disinfectant and there he'll stay till I fish him out.' Once again she had forgotten herself, and we carried the smell of manure around all day, causing a few jocular remarks all round.

We got underway once more, noting with pleasure the green tipped buds on the chestnuts and oaks and the early spring daffodils decorating the village gardens. We were very busy on this particular day, and as we progressed I found for some reason that I had a lot of books left which wouldn't go on the shelves. I wondered how to dispose of them as I hadn't time to 'weed' the shelves and take off odd ones to fit others in. I pressed my readers to take more than their usual quota, and this dealt with some of them, but at the last stop I had still about 40 or 50 left. Then into the van came the local vicar's wife, a very sweet but gullible person, who peered at me over the top of her horn rimmed specs.

'I'm in rather a hurry today, dear, can you help me choose some books quickly, oh, and have you any of the ones my sister asked for?'

Suddenly, I had an idea – a very unprofessional to be sure but the sight of the unsuspecting Mrs Eland spurred me on.

'Why I've got some of your kind of books right here, take plenty of these.' And so saying, I hastily began to take tickets from the piles of books I had left. Thick and fast I piled them into her waiting arms.

'Just a moment, I think I'll have enough here.' she said mildly.

'Oh but these others are for your sister, the ones she ordered.' I lied – sincerely hoping her sister would miss us next time. Mrs Eland was staggering under the pile of murders, romances and war tales – hardly the choice of a vicar's wife, rather my choice for her.

'Oh dear,' she exclaimed, 'I don't think I can manage all these, I must go and get the vicar to come and help me.'

Dumping the pile of books on my desk, she disappeared, to return a few minutes later with the unfortunate vicar and a large cardboard box. Whilst she was away I took the opportunity to slip another dozen or so books on to the pile.

At the sight of the vicar I couldn't surpress a smile. He was a fat jocular man, but very small with a shiny face which beamed at me over the top of the cardboard box. I hastily piled the books into the box, and watched his legs sag under the weight.

'Really Emily,' he said mildly, 'you've got rather a lot here haven't you this time?'

'Well,' Mrs Eland blinked, 'really, Mrs Moore has been too kind in giving me all these but . . .'

I interrupted her with loud assurances that she was quite welcome to the books, and would enjoy them I hoped, whereupon she thrust a bunch of daffodils into my hand and helped prevent the vicar from falling into the box head first. I felt rather mean as I watched them go, especially in view of the flowers, but Bill was delighted,

'Best way of getting rid of books I've ever seen,' he exclaimed.

We carried on to the next stop and then we stopped. Bill decided to put some water into the radiator as it was rather dry. Several readers looked in the van whilst he was doing this and I chatted amiably with them all. Just as the last customer left, a Mrs Burns, came rushing in, her arms full of books and her face full of concern.

'Are you leaking?' she cried.

'Am I what?!' I replied, astonished.

'Well, there's water running from under your van all over the road, and I thought maybe one of you had overflowed.'

I laughed and explained the situation to her.

'Have you a rum book?' she asked coyly. 'There's nothing like a rum book when you can't sleep at night.'

'Well,' I hesitated, 'what exactly do you mean?'

'What's he reading?' she asked, nodding at Bill, 'he always gets the rum ones.'

Bill blushed and said he only read general books, but Mrs Burns' eyes twinkled and she winked at me.

'I'll take your choice today,' she muttered, and he eventually rallied to the cause and chose her a novel.

We continued on our way, chatting to our eager readers as they scurried in and out like busy bees, choosing their books and rushing back to their little cottages which gleamed brightly in the spring sunshine. We stopped outside Mrs Baron's cottage on the outskirts of Abbey Village, and I jumped from the van to admire her lovely garden, ablaze with forsythia, daffodils, crocus and budding tulips. It really was a picture, and just then Mrs Baron herself, a wrinkled old lady of 82, appeared at the cottage door.

'Come in dear, and have a cup of tea,' she said, 'I've a plate of freshly baked scones here.'

I sadly declined the invitation explaining that we were rather short of time and had to hurry on, but not for the first time did I marvel that an old lady of that age could manage to do all she did without any help. Her garden certainly did her credit all the year round.

Our last stop of the day was at a quaint old cottage with the intriguing name of 'Witches Den' inhabited by a sweet but rather eccentric lady by the name of Miss Letitia Longbottom. I usually chose books for her as her eyesight was not very good and I took care to choose books with as large a print as possible. She was given to rather wild expressions, and as I anticipated, entered the van exclaiming, 'Hello darlings, how nice to see you.' Bill usually put his head into his book and read fervently on as Miss Letitia gushed forth.

'Have you got me some good ones, sweetie?' she asked me. I pushed a pile of books towards her.

'Oh thank you so much darling,' she enthused, 'these books are simply delicious, oh you are so sweet to choose them for me.'

I blushed as I always did over her profuse expressions, and murmured that it had been a lovely day.

'Absolutely perfect,' she agreed. 'Have you got anything new by Jean Plaidy, I absolutely adore her books my dear?'

Eventually after much 'darling' and 'dearing' she left the van, and we were able to get back to base on time.

Cottages on Overshores Road, between the reservoirs at Entwistle

The next day was similar to its predecessors, lots of little stops to make in two villages, and several farms to visit all around Entwistle. When we had had our dinner after a rather uneventful morning, and were passing the small railway station at one of the villages over Wayoh Reservoir, I decided to go into the ladies room and have a wash and tidy up. This I duly did, whilst Bill stopped the van and dutifully waited in the station yard.

I popped into the loo whilst I was there, but on trying to get out again, I found that the blessed door was stuck. I pushed and pushed, kicked and banged, but all to no avail; the door was firmly stuck! I looked around the loo, there was no window, just three brick walls and a very thick door. What a predicament! I shouted until I was hoarse, but no one heard. There were three other rooms before you reached the station platform, and of course being only a rural service, relatively few people used it.

For fifteen minutes I tried desperately to make myself heard with no result. The only hope was that eventually Bill would realise that something was wrong and come to my rescue. Eventually, after half an hour had passed, I heard the outer door slam and footsteps approaching the toilet door. Bill's voice boomed out:

'Is that you Benita, are you in there?'

'Yes its me' I muttered thankfully, 'can you push the door, its stuck?'

'You silly twit, fancy getting stuck in a loo!!' said Bill. 'Hang on, I'll get you out in a jiffy.'

Bill pushed manfully at the offending door, but it refused to budge.

'I'll have to bring the porter,' he shouted, quite unnecessarily, as I was right behind the door. 'Won't be a minute,' he said and went off.

Ten minutes passed, then twenty; I was beginning to worry. Suddenly, I heard footsteps and Bill's voice said:

'I've found the porter, cleaning out his Beehive, that's why it's taken so long.'

The porter's voice floated over to me, calm and reassuring:

'Don't worry love, have you out of there in a jiffy, I will.'

Keys jangled in the lock, and any minute I expected the door to open and release me, but no such luck.

'Sorry love,' said the porter, 'my key won't turn, seems its a bit bent like, I'll have to go for Jock – he's the signalman, you know.'

I was desperately frustrated and also worried about our work time-table. 'If this goes on much longer I'll be here all day,' I thought. The porter trooped off, presumably to find the signalman, and Bill stayed outside the door trying to cheer me up.

'You're a one,' he said, 'fancy being stuck here for so long.' He began to sing 'Three old ladies locked in a lavatory' but I was not amused.

'Its the last time I'm coming to a railway station loo, anyway!' I exclaimed.

After what seemed like eternity, the porter arrived complete with the signalman and his keys, and finally, after a two-hour vigil, I was released.

'My, you've had a long wait,' said the porter. 'Sorry I took so long, but Jock here,' he indicated the amused signalman, 'was just brewing up, so I had a cup with him.'

I was livid. 'If there'd been a rail disaster here,' I grumbled, 'would everything have had to wait for your cups of tea?'

But the men just grinned and sauntered off to their respective jobs.

"You silly twit, fancy getting stuck in a loo!"

'Don't worry,' said Bill, 'we'll soon make up for lost time.' And we did, and a great deal of amusement was caused by my brief but explicit explanation to our waiting readers of Chapeltown Road as to why we were so late. Later, as I told my husband of the ordeal, I saw the funny side of it all.

As spring advanced, so the countryside become more beautiful. Fields became rich with marsh marigolds and daisies cascaded down the moors as we trundled on our way. Colourful banks of celandines were arrayed on every side and my heart rejoiced as the beauties of nature unfolded before us. Spirits became noticeably brighter, and even our grumpy old farmer, Mr. Newton, a man noted for his depressing views on life, rejoiced in the mellow spring sunshine. It is always a joy for me to watch the progress of trees and flowers at this time of year, and this year the countryside seemed to be even more bountiful. Perhaps it was because I was enjoying my work so much, and meeting such interesting people, that everything seemed brighter, who can tell? Anyway, I certainly enjoyed my days out, and there always seemed to be some new adventure round the corner.

One rather murky day, after completing our rounds, we were approaching the outskirts of Bolton and Astley Bridge on our way home, when suddenly, as we stopped at some traffic lights, to my astonishment smoke began to pour into the cab of the library van. For a moment I sat there stupified, then it suddenly dawned on me. We were on fire! Bill didn't seem to have noticed anything until he suddenly began to cough.

'We're on fire!' I yelled. Bill, startled, stopped the engine and jumped out of the cab.

'Call the Fire Brigade!' he yelled at me. I got out of the van and looked around. Dogs barked, children shrieked and a crowd of chattering women appeared on the pavement as if by magic.

'Where's the nearest 'phone?' I asked one of them.

There's a butcher's just along there,' said one, 'he'll let you use his 'phone.'

I rushed into the astonished butcher's shop, and panted out a request to use his 'phone. He pointed into the back, and I pushed my way between the frozen carcasses of meat and dialed 999. After calling the Fire Brigade, I also 'phoned our Librarian in Ramsbottom, who advised me to contact the vehicle maintenance unit at headquarters. I rushed back to the van and saw Bill's legs sticking out from underneath.

'Are you okay?' I shouted at him. Bill emerged greasy and perspiring from beneath the van.

'Looks like a wiring fault,' he said; 'the fire isn't serious, it will probably be out before anyone arrives'. He was right, too, for a few minutes later the Fire Brigade arrived and pronounced that there had been a fire in the electrical circuit which was almost extinguished. Just to make sure, however, they squirted foam under the van, much to the delight of the gathering of children who had flooded to the scene.

The van, however, although now fully extinguished, could not be moved until the mechanics arrived, and as it was almost six o'clock by this time, Bill suggested that I had better set off home. This, however, was easier said than done! I was some twenty miles from my home town and as the local bus service was rather erratic I wondered what to do.

At that moment however, I spotted the van of a cooked meat and pie firm who had their factory some two miles from my home town. I had the idea of asking the driver for a lift and Bill came with me to explain the situation. The driver being a gallant gentleman agreed to rescue me, and after an interesting tour of all the pie shops in the area, I arrived home some two hours later – a weary, dishevelled and somewhat daunted mobile librarian.

And so the days continued, each bringing its own pleasures, trials and tribulations.Every day (or so it seemed to me) the countryside became more alive and bountiful. Pussy willows abounded everywhere, and little shoots of green thrust their way upwards towards the sky. The hedgerows were spangled with baby buds and, as April ended, tiny buds of Lilac appeared, first a delicate lavender, then purpling to a rich deep blue. Early horse chestnut trees began to open their sticky buds and shake out their delicate silky leaves – like children dancing. The fields and meadows were verdant green with new grass and I considered myself very lucky to have the opportunity to see all these wonders of nature.

In the spring, a young man's (or in this case woman's) fancy lightly turns to thoughts of love, so the poets tell us. Whether or not it was the spring, the sap rising, or some other wild explanation I do not know, but something had certainly upset Miss Scarlett Sandys' equilibrium. As soon as she entered the van she would make gay, coy remarks and flutter her eyelashes at Bill, asking his advice in lieu of mine, and generally claiming his attention as much as she could.

At first Bill was rather flattered by this extoling of his manly virtues, but after a while the newness wore off and he grumpily retired to the back of the van whilst I served Miss Scarlett. However, unabashed by Bill's attitude she continued her assault for quite a number of visits,coming into the van on each occasion quite gaily and erratically dressed and with a large loop of beads swinging round her neck and breasts. I wondered if she wore her scarlet bloomers underneath, and said the same to Bill, who laughed and said she probably never cast them off even in a heatwave.

Eventually, however, as spring advanced and Bill didn't respond to her affection, Miss Scarlett reverted to her old intrepid self.

'Having her last fling, no doubt,' remarked Bill, when it became obvious that he dare speak naturally to her again.

The spring had clearly had a cheering effect on all our readers, as tender, green young leaves appeared and the lambs became frisky in the meadows. The demand for lighthearted novels and stories became much more marked and we had to renew our stock of this particular type of book. I found myself becoming more and more involved in the lives and happenings of our readers. Indeed spring seemed to have had a remarkable effect not only on Miss Scarlett Sandys but also on Tommy Riley who 'spring cleaned' his Gladstone bag to the extent of putting clean newspaper in the bottom!

It was one of the lovliest springs I remember, with bluebells making a sweet-smelling carpet under fresh green beech leaves and small clumps of primroses and violets nestling on the side of fresh, sparkling streams – a far cry from their poor polluted town sisters. Because we traversed many of the remote spots, little known and visited, we could see the beauty of the countryside in its true state, a thing which I fear is becoming more an more rare. I felt sorry for the town children who missed all these little delights.

Little Mrs Miller from 'The limes' came in one morning and gave me a bunch of cowslips, lovely and slender. I thanked her warmly and she asked if we could choose some books for her aunt who was staying with her, and who, for some strange reason declined, to come to the van herself. I was asking what kind of books she liked, when the body herself appeared in the doorway and with difficulty mounted the steps. Tall, gaunt and horsey-looking, she smelt strongly of something I couldn't quite christen but which was probably 'ashes of tom cat' or some such thing.

'I thought you weren't coming in, Aunty,' said Mrs Miller.

'I decided I'd better choose my own books after all,' she stated. Then, looking scornfully at me, 'I can't be sure she'd choose summat to my taste with all this literature about today.'

I felt my cheeks burn slightly, but bent my head and worked hard at the tickets so that Aunt Agatha (I believe that was her name) couldn't see she'd upset me. She browsed around for four or five minutes then turned up at the desk with a John Braine book; hardly my choice for her, and after what she'd said hardly her choice I would have imagined. However, there it was and after a few more words with Mrs Miller, Aunt Agatha stalked out of the van, her head high in the air.

Mrs Miller was most apologetic.

'I'm sorry Mrs Moore; she's not bad really but she has an awful haughty attitude and can't help saying the wrong thing. Actually I dread her coming to stay, but I suppose I must do my duty and have her in turn like everyone else.'

I sympathised with Mrs Miller and said I quite understood.

'We get all types in here,' I said, 'but thank goodness 98% are very nice people like yourself.' Thus reassured, Mrs Miller went back to her house and her tetchy aunt.

Chapter Eight

Gardening

THE fields around Belmont were a riot of marsh marigolds and May flowers and, for want of a better utensil, Bill's teapot was pressed into service as I picked huge bunches to take back home with us. It looked grotesquely funny and, with flowers dumped in the top and draped round the spout, it stood on my shelf next to the tickets for all to see and admire. Then, as nodding buttercups replaced the marigolds, they too succumbed to the teapot, and eventually to my vases at home.

As the days sped by, the mellow spring rolled into early summer, and the cottage gardens became a blaze of colour. Many of my readers shared my interest in flowers and nature and I had not a few interesting conversations with them, and picked up many useful tips for my own garden.

When the readers learned of my enthusiasm for plants and flowers I was inundated with pot plants, cuttings and roots in each place the van visited. In fact, the van became a regular swap shop of plants and cuttings. Readers in neighbouring villages would bring in parcels of roots, and, after safely depositing their romances or westerns in their bags, would whisper furtively to me:

"Would you give this to Mrs So and So of such house, I know she needs some of these cuttings."

I duly obliged when I could and Mrs So and So would reciprocate by sending a pot plant back to the sender next time.

One such body who was very fond of her garden was Mrs Fairburn of Oakwood cottages – a delightful character who, with her long grey coat and wispy white hair rather resembled the grey rabbit in Alison Uttley's books. She grew the most gorgeous flowers, and very kindly treated Bill and myself to a bunch on our visits. One day she entered the van with a large parcel of roots, and asked us to give them to Mrs Reeves in the next village. Now Mrs Reeves, was one of the few readers that I didn't look forward to seeing, mainly because she talked so much that she always made us an hour late on our schedule.

I politely asked her to leave once or twice, but it seemed to me to do no good, so I tried to think of some other means of discouraging her chatter. So, of course, I knew that if I gave the parcel from Mrs Fairburn to her, we would have a long saga on the powers of rooting powder or something of the sort, so I resolved to stop this if I could. Knowing Mrs Reeves as I did, I realised that this would be easier said than done, but I decided to tell her that they had to be planted at once or they would wilt.

We arrived at the next village and, true to form, Mrs Reeves was holding forth on some trivial subject to some readers who heralded our arrival with delight as a means of escape. On entering the van, Mrs Reeves spent about five minutes saying how she liked us being on time, and when I could get a word in edgeways, I told her about the roots from Mrs Fairburn, and how quickly they needed to be planted.

Mrs. Reeves, however, did not take the hint and gaily rambled on about something and nothing. At length, after all the other readers had gone and we were already overdue at the next stop, I said to Mrs Reeves:

'These roots will be dead if you don't get them planted at once.'

This seemed to rattle Mrs Reeves, for she drew herself up to her full height and said curtly:

'Let me tell you, I was planting roots before you were born and don't need your advice on things.'

After saying this she picked up her books and the roots and marched airily out of the van. This episode did some good, though, as we didn't see her again for almost a month but when she did come again she was as bad as ever and I resigned myself to putting up with her forever.

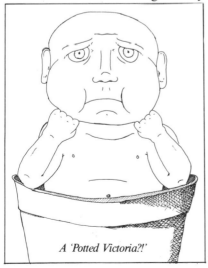

A 'Potted Victoria?!'

I was delighted to exchange plants and cuttings with my readers and was always anxious to pick up ideas and hear of new species. One day, however, I made a rather amusing mistake. Two of my readers were talking in the van when a third member, a young housewife called Mrs Billett, came rushing in.

'My goodness,' she exclaimed, 'I thought I was going to miss you so I just potted Victoria, grabbed my books and ran out.'

'Potted Victoria,' I asked, 'is that a new species of flower?'

Mrs Billet laughed till the tears ran down her cheeks and the other readers pricked up their ears at the commotion.

'No, I mean I've just sat my daughter, Victoria, on her potty then I could come out to you!' We all laughed at my mistake, including Bill who had been eavesdropping throughout.

One of the best gardeners of all was an elderly widow by the name of Julia Tump who owned a sprawling allotment behind her small terraced house. Her garden was magnificent. Everything she turned her hand to or planted seemed to flourish abundantly. Talk about green fingers, she knew every trick of the trade and I spent many a happy ten minutes or so listening to her hints and admiring her flowers.

As my passion for flowers grew, so did my readers' generosity and I was overwhelmed by the masses of plants which mysteriously appeared in the van. Luckily, Bill was also a keen gardener and readers included him in the general exchange of plants and tips. One day, however, an incident occurred which rather dampened his enthusiasm. We were visiting Edgworth village when nice Mrs Fowler entered the van. During the time I was speaking to her the conversation turned to gardening and, on finding that I was a keen gardener, she offered to give me two hydrangea plants which she had no room for. Delighted at this offer, I asked Bill if he would go and bring them whilst I attended to our other customers. Bill agreed and set off with Mrs Fowler back to her house.

A quarter of an hour passed, then half an hour, and I was just beginning to wonder what had happened when I saw Bill staggering across the road with a huge hyndrangea in each hand, his face was bright red and beads of sweat ran down his face.

'Bill!' I exclaimed, 'whatever is the matter?'

'Stupid woman,' he growled as he savagely tossed the unfortunate plants into the van. 'She said they needed digging out, but she didn't tell me that they were each stuck in a dolly tub,' he said, and drove off in a fury. It was only when he calmed down later that he would explain.

'I went into the garden,' he said 'and there's these two hydrangeas each in one of those old' dolly tubs. Talk about being root-bound, I think she put cement in, not soil!'

It appeared that each plant was so firmly rooted that Bill couldn't budge them, and only after a terrific struggle did he succeed in pulling them out, causing him to perspire profusely. Of course, I saw the funny side of this, but Bill was annoyed with my laughter and remained in a huff for the rest of the day.

*   *   *

The post office at Edgworth, one of our busiest villages

Large patches of aubretia blazed in the sunshine, candytuft and virginia stock sprouted everywhere, the rows of neat terraced houses and the cottages with their gardens brightened our day as we went about our rounds. Early June was rather cold but the days were filled with pleasure, for me at any rate, as we rambled through the villages and from cottage to cottage. The farms and their animals were also of great interest and I have great admiration for the farmers' wives who find time to do so much work and still enjoy life. We frequently benefited from our trips to farms, to the tune of fresh eggs, warm from the nest, fruit freshly picked and many other delights such as townspeople never know exist.

I was surprised to find that farmers, who are such busy people, find time to read at all, but they did, as I found by experience. In fact, some farmers, would often take as many as twenty or thirty books for their families. One farmer's wife, however, went a bit too far. She would take half the van if you didn't stop her. Trouble was she was such a pleasant person, that I found it hard to reprimand her. She would enter the van with a huge cardboard box and begin to fill it as soon as I'd taken the returned books out. Luckily I hit upon a method of restriction without her knowing. She was a prolific talker and Bill would engage her attention upon a subject and I would quietly take out and craftily place some of the books from her box under the counter without her noticing. All this worked well, until one day she turned round and caught me at it. I hastened to explain that we were short of books and I think she took the hint because she never took quite so many again.

Part of our route took us by the side of several reservoirs near Edgworth owned by the local water authority, and the scenery surrounding them was really lovely. Rolling moors in the background and strong straight fir and pine trees planted by the waterside. Bill and I would often sit and have our lunch by the water's edge whenever we could. Bill Burton was the water Bailiff and he used to tell us of the days gone by when the local squire owned all the land, before it was compulsorily bought. However, I can honestly say that the intervention of man has done a great deal of good in this case at any rate. It was very relaxing to sit up above the reservoirs and watch the wild life on the water below. One day, as I was strolling along a lane in the new part, I looked over a hedge and was delighted to see a small pond on which floated a mother moorhen and her young. Every time we went that way I made a point of visiting the moorhen family and taking along some titbits for them.

If we were lucky, we sometimes spotted a small stoat or weasel as it dodged from the hedge when we rumbled by. As each new day dawned, it brought with it some new and enchanting aspects of the countryside which I was fortunate enough to witness. I can see now, in my mind's eye, the delights of nature and her marvellous work. Whoever says that Lancashire has no lovely scenery has never trodden the paths that I have. I could expound for hours on the joy which I experienced as each village and piece of countryside became familiar to me. However, I must continue my narrative.

One Thursday, I think it was, we had just visited Miss Marigold Mashom, who looked very dashing in a new lavender jumper and a tweed skirt, when Mrs Evans, one of our farmer's wives, hailed us from the side of the road.

'Would you mind calling at Rookery Nook before you come down to us this afternoon – about 2 pm? It's just down the lane before you turn up to our farm?'

Always eager for new custom, I thanked Mrs Evans and agreed to call.

'Funny,' I said to Bill, as we trundled on, 'I've never noticed the lane before.'

'I have,' replied Bill, 'but I always thought it was a cul-de-sac, and that nobody lived down there.'

Promptly at 2 pm we bumped down the lane to Rookery Nook which turned out to be an old gipsy caravan converted into a permanent home complete with garden, gate and nameplate. Mrs Tabitha Snape was pleased to see us.

'How kind of you to come,' she exclaimed, 'I do love books and didn't know your service existed until Mrs Evans mentioned it the other day.'

As she was speaking I took a good look at Mrs Snape and decided she must have been a real gipsy at some time. Her slightly greying hair was long, black and curly and she must have looked very handsome when she was younger. She wore long jangly earrings, three links of beads, and bracelets on both arms.

'I wonder if she still reads crystal balls or tea-leaves,' I mused as she browsed round our shelves. It appeared that Mrs Snape's great passion was birds, wild or otherwise. She had a few cages dotted about her garden and the caravan was surrounded by trees which were absolutely choked with large nests (presumably rooks and crows) – hence the name Rookery Nook. I was very interested and asked Mrs. Snape all about her birds. It appeared that the cages were for wild birds that she found who had hurt themselves, and she put them in the cages until she nursed them back to health. Today, they were all in the garden 'taking the air'.

Mrs. Snape certainly must have had a way with birds for as we spoke to her a tame magpie hovered outside the van and a jackdaw perched on the gate, whilst in the distance on the grass, a group of crows and rooks eyed me speculatively as I came with Mrs. Snape to the door. She asked me to get her as many books on birds as I could, and I gladly complied. I looked forward to our visits to Rookery Nook with relish for Mrs Snape was certainly a very interesting character.

'We do meet them don't we?' I said to Bill, and smiling he agreed.

Chapter Nine

Election Day

I T WAS at the end of May when the local elections were held in the various villages up and down our area, and to my surprise the villagers seemed to take a lively interest in the affair.

For weeks before, we could see notices displayed in cottage windows, village shops and more prominent places, blatantly urging the villagers to vote for so and so, and for about two weeks before in every village where we stopped, the names of local candidates were on everyone's lips. In fact we witnessed some very heated exchanges in our van at times. Stout Tory farmers would argue with the Labour opponents, whilst many of the older people looked back to the days when the Liberal party was at its height. Many a friendly neighbour would overnight become a bitter enemy because of politics.

In one village, when we arrived the day after polling day, there was great excitement. Apparently two local farmers who were candidates had polled the same number of votes, and they had to draw their names out of a hat to see who would be elected. One farmer was the retiring councillor, and the other a newcomer. The retiring councillor swore that he should keep the seat, and when the other man's name was drawn out of the hat, he refused to accept the decision. He threatened to appeal against it, and also to ruin his opponent as regards stock and land. All this was narrated to me at great length by Miss Martha Rose, who exclaimed in a stentorian voice, 'I doesn't know what things is coming to.'

One day, when polling was actually taking place in one of the villages, we arrived at the local pub, just in time to hear a heated exchange between two ancient villagers.

'I'm voting for Tom Brown,' said one.

'Then thas a reet nitwit,' said the other. 'Dusta not know he only wants to get on t'council so as he can have a council house.'

'That's a lie,' answered the first.

'Tis not,' said the other.

This went on for some time, with the landlord standing listening to all this rigmarole, until I gently reminded him that we were waiting for him. Just as we went through the door, one of the old men raised his pint of beer and threw it over the other man. I really think they would have started a fight if the landlord hadn't have stepped out, whereupon they both turned on him and said he was to blame.

'You can't win with these lot,' he said, wiping beer from his jacket, 'they think I'm a foreigner and I've been here twenty years.'

I expressed sympathy for him and led him to the van outside.

If you can see what effect local elections have on normally calm and friendly people, then you can imagine the excitement that a parliamentary by-election caused. A by-election was to be held in the rural seat of Mosley, due to the death of its member. We set out for various villages in the area knowing full well that polling was taking place, but little prepared for what we found. Many of the villagers sported rosettes, some of the men even wore ties in the colour of the party of their choice. There were many furtive conversations and sly nods and winks between villagers, as men of opposing views loudly proclaimed their loyalties. Even Miss Scarlett and Miss Opal Sandys seemed engulfed by the excitement and twittered merrily to us about their favourite party. I think the thoughts of the election had put thoughts of books and their authors and titles out of some people's minds. One old woman came up to me and said, 'Have you got a piece of string – or else?'

'Whatever for?' I asked (secretly wondering if her knickers had snapped!)

'What for?' she mocked; 'I want to read it tha silly young doll!'

'But I don't know anything about a piece of string,' I said, 'or else what?' I added as an afterthought.

'Or else I'll report thee if tha doesn't stop talking daft,' she replied. 'I tell thee I want a piece of string!'

Eventually, it dawned on me, what she wanted was a book called *A rope in case.* 'So much for 'or else" I muttered as I found her the book.

That day villagers poured into the van, arguing about politics and who would get in etc. Being rather interested in politics myself, I threw in a question or two just to hear them argue about it. In the end, it turned out that an independent outsider won the seat, thus causing more upset and chatter in the villages. It was not just friendly banter though, the villagers were in deadly earnest and clung doggedly to their own views. In fact, later that day, we visited the home of Tory Councillor Mrs V. Holt, who was in tears because the local youths (strongly Labour apparently) had pulled up her precious Honeysuckle because of their opposition to the Tory party. Mrs Holt was very upset, but I promised to get her another cutting of Honeysuckle for our next visit, which I duly did.

The by-election surprise result caused endless amazement and for weeks afterwards we could still hear the locals giving their version as to what went wrong.

'I say the count must have been wrong,' stated Miss Grace Atterton.

'Votes been tampered with,' said Old Ben Tin (so called because of his tin leg).

'Rubbish,' said Mrs Cleever (whose husband held a local government post), 'you can't interfere with democracy you know.'

And so it went on, day in and day out (many of our villages were in the constituency) until a fierce fire broke out at one of the mills in the largest village and the mill was burned down to the ground, then our readers speculated about the possibility of arson. Apparently it had cost quite a number of people their jobs, and there was great anxiety amongst the villagers as to how they could now earn their living. As it transpired, a number of them did find jobs locally, but many had to travel into the nearest town for work, a fact which caused great unhappiness, as they had loved working locally. The more sensible, however, counted themselves lucky to have found a job and still be able to live in their home village.

A rather fat, jocular spinster with the whimsical name of Pearl Barley, came bouncing in after the news of the fire, and slapped me on the back very heartily. Indeed, so mighty was her hand, that she sent a tray of reader's tickets flying over the floor, and a gust of wind blew them through the door so that I had to scamper after them.

'Sorry about that,' she said jauntily. 'Have you heard about the fire? A good thing if you ask me, the place was nearly a ruin anyway, so it's time it came down.'

Obviously, as her livelihood was not affected, she could take a more optimistic view, but I didn't think much of her carefree attitude about other peoples' jobs and told her so, whereupon she marched out of the van in a huff.

Mrs Alice Edmundson and Benita Moore exchanging books at her farm on Halcombe Road

Chapter Ten

Summer Holidays

AND so the days rolled by. A cold June changed into a brilliant July, and as the local 'Wakes weeks' or town holidays drew nearer, so my readers became noticeably more lighthearted and cheerful. Not all the villages were on holiday at the same time, and so we continued our service throughout the summer, with the exception of two weeks holiday which Bill and myself took.

One bright July day, we were travelling towards Belmont village when the van suddenly started to cough and splutter. After a few tense moments, Bill decided it was only a lack of petrol which had caused us to stop – he had forgotten to get some that morning. There we were, miles from anywhere.

'What are we going to do?' asked Bill.

There was only one thing for it, Bill, taking a petrol tin with him, set off for the nearest garage, and hoped to get a lift along the way. After two refusals a car did eventually stop and I saw him safely off.

Meanwhile, I decided to use the spare time available by putting the books into good order. I'd been working for about twenty minutes when I heard faint scratchings outside the van. At first I thought I must be imagining things but as it continued I decided to investigate. I opened the van door and to my horror came face to face (or rather eye to eye) with a huge black bull. I shut the door as quickly as possible, my heart pounding, if there's one thing I'm afraid of it's bulls.

However, after my first fears had subsided a little, my courage returned, and I decided that something must be done if the van was to be kept free from scratches. Gingerly I opened the door and peered out. The bull was still there and eyed me coldly – it had obviously taken an instant dislike to me and snorted into my face, covering me with saliva. I wondered what to do for the best. Then suddenly an idea came to me; I would creep around from the driver's door and lure the bull away from the van. How does one lure a bull? I checked our books on bullfighting and the only one we had said, 'The bull must be attracted by means of gesticulations or other methods.' This presumably meant a red cloth and as I hadn't got one, I decided it would have to be wild gesticulations.

Taking my courage in both hands, I slowly edged my way round the front of the van. The bull was still there brushing against the side and chewing steadily, its tail lashing to and fro. How was I to begin? I decided to try a 'subtle' approach and call it away. What sort of noise does one use to call a bull? I mused. The book gave me no clue about

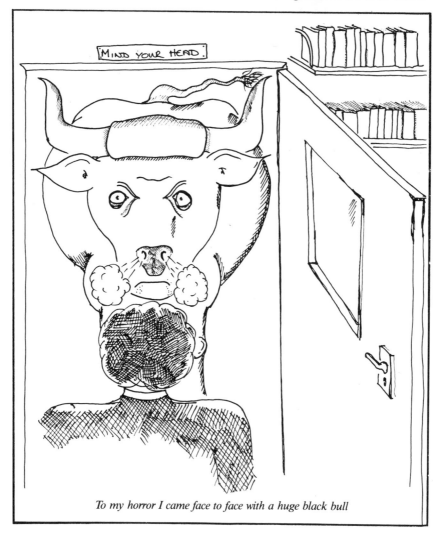

To my horror I came face to face with a huge black bull

this, so I began calling softly: 'Here boy, come on boy, here.' The bull didn't move an inch – this was obviously the wrong approach. I tried again, a bit louder this time – still no effect. Action was needed, so I picked up a small stone and threw it deftly at the bulls ear, it blinked back, obviously astonished at my behaviour, but still it didn't move.

I tried again, this time fiercely wiggling my ears and making a loud hissing noise. Nothing happened, and I secretly cursed the bullfighting book. I resolved to try just once more. I was engaged in making more wild gesticulations, when I was suddenly shocked by a deep voice behind me.

'And what do you think you're doing?'

I felt a real fool, I can tell you. It was the farmer and he'd been watching me and had come to collect his animal. I blushed furiously and began to explain. The farmer chuckled.

'Don't you be afraid of old Napoleon there,' he said, 'wouldn't harm a fly, he wouldn't'

I looked doubtfully at Napoleon, who by now was grazing peacefully nearby. The farmer's eyes twinkled behind his glasses.

'Don't you worry now lass there's no harm done.' he said.

I explained why the van was in the lane, and after he'd been assured that I wasn't going to trespass on his land, he led the animal away. With just one snap of his fingers, the old bull obediently trotted after him as docile as a lamb. I looked on, feeling very foolish. I returned to my work and shortly afterwards Bill arrived with the petrol. When I told him of the incident, he roared with laughter.

'Get yourself into some pickles don't you?' he said.

We arrived at Belmont some time later. It was a pretty little village composed of two long rows of houses, one on each side of the high street. These houses all had different coloured doors and paint work and really looked quite gay. There was a local legend in the village about some mysterious 'treacle mines' which were supposed to have existed some hundreds of years ago on the moors some miles away, near Tockholes village as well as at Belmont. In fact the 'treacle mines' had become a local joke, and all unsuspecting newcomers were told to go and search for them (without success of course). It is surprising how many people fall for the trick and set off over the moors in earnest looking for the mines. One young man is reputed to have set off on the search and never came back at all, much to the chagrin of his fiancée, and no more was ever heard of him at all. However, the 'mines' have certainly made Belmont village well-known, and at Easter and other holidays hundreds of people flock to the village to make a search and also to sail on the famous 'Blue Lagoon', a local reservoir near Winter Hill. Belmont also possesses a lovely old seventeeth–century church which has been very well preserved. All the villagers are very proud of it and delighted in relating tales of its origin to me. Unfortunately there was a dubious character by the nickname of 'Dirty Lizzie', who frequented the churchyard, and if not watched was liable to do damage. Dirty Lizzie was one of our customers and she represented one great problem to me. Whether or not it was due to frequenting the tombstones, or whether she lived with mice or rats I can't say – but she smelt dreadful! Her face was black, her clothes old and filthy and I don't think she ever had a bath or washed. When she came into the van in the hot summer weather, she made the place smell awful, and all the other readers would remove themselves either by going outside, or to the extreme opposite end of the van.

It really was a problem, I didn't know what to do. I couldn't refuse her books as she always returned them and didn't dirty them, miraculously enough, but so many of my readers complained that I felt that something must be done. She was big and fat and flabby and as we watched, her tummy bounced around like a football. However, luck was on my side. Come one unusually hot day, she sailed into the van to choose her books and was just sailing out again when she tripped on the top step and went flying, books and all. I rushed to her assistance, but she would have none of my help and perversely marched off to her cottage. When she didn't appear two weeks later, we learned that she had broken a bone in her ankle and was refusing to come to the van again. I sent her some books via a neighbour, and thereafter she continued to use the neighbour's service, thus relieving the van of her stench, and me of a very awkward problem.

Summer holidays were the topic of conversation. We heard a constant hubub of holiday chatter from readers who had been away, and excited murmurings from those who were going soon. It appeared that places such as Torquay and Llandudno were firm favourites, in the villages that we visited at any rate. Some readers even sent cards to the library for Bill and myself; that was just like north country folk, warm and friendly, as always.

In early August one of our readers' sons was due to be married and as a joke, his farmer neighbour asked me for a book on marriage guidance to give him as a present. As it happened, we hadn't a book in the van on that subject, but I did, however, find one called *How to be a Father*. The farmer asked me to give it to the bridegroom's mother. She was very amused, but not so her son, who accused us of interfering.

One of our readers, a Mrs Simpson, ran a small tea garden near the 'Strawbury Duck' pub, which was very popular with the visitors. When we arrived one Tuesday, she was holding a garden party, and invited us to join in. Not being suitably dressed I politely declined. Maybe it's just as well we didn't go, as we heard later that a farmer nearby had been spreading manure over his fields, and as the wind was prevailing it wafted into Mrs Simpson's garden, much to the disgust of her guests, who departed with speed.

The fields were now ablaze with scarlet poppies and white marguerites. There was the smell of fresh hay and fruit everywhere and I eagerly looked forward to each day spent on the van. Days seemed to fly past and I became more and more attached to my friends the readers. One person to whom I was not very attached, however, was a Mrs Dodds, a cantankerous, middle-aged lady, who insisted on keeping all the books required by other readers. When our readers requested a book, we 'stopped' it in the issue, and asked the person who had it out to return it as soon as possible. Mrs Dodds was a villain, she hoarded books like an old magpie and we had a terrible job to get them back from her. No matter how politely I asked her, she always declined to return them. I had several arguments with her on this subject, and in the end threatened to withdraw her membership if she didn't comply. After this threat she was better, but refused to speak to me on any visit for several months. I can honestly say that this was the only real unpleasantness we had with any of our readers, thank goodness.

The mellow summer days continued, a mixture for me of joy in its delights and sadness in its passing. During the summer holidays we were beseiged by the children who were normally at school, but who now hailed our arrival with as much delight as the ice-cream van. They seemed to relish rummaging through our selection of children's books, which although not very large, was as varied as we could possibly make it.

The children who inhabited the farms seemed to be the most appreciative of our service, and the most friendly too. They charged into the van, frequently bringing their pets with them. Mice and rabbits were quite welcome, but I drew the line at goats, who made a beeline for the books, presumably regarding them as a new delicacy. The farmers' wives during this, their busiest season, bustled in and out of the van like busy bees, hardly finding time to choose their usual quota of romances and murders. I noted with delight the farm activities, the fields full of sweet smelling hay, and all the enchanting sights and sounds of the Lancashire countryside.

One day which was rather cold, Bill and I ate our sandwiches indoors. We had the door and windows tightly closed, and were practically immune to all outside activity as we ate and talked. Suddenly I glanced up, sensing that something was amiss. On looking through the van window, I saw that we were surrounded by a herd of cows who nestled and nudged each other as they flocked around our van. What fatal attraction we had for them I shall never know but they certainly made a beeline for us, as it appeared the whole herd had descended upon us. I opened the door and one cow immediately poked its head inside and would have ventured to climb the steps if I hadn't discouraged it by poking a brush at its legs. Bill sounded the horn in an effort to frighten the animals away, but the cows had no intention of moving, they remained silent as ever, pushing and nosing around the van. We were due to set off to our next stop, but couldn't move an inch, so we just had to sit tight and wait until the cows decided to move of their own accord.

Fifteen minutes went by, then twenty, and still the cows milled round the van. How long we would have remained there I cannot say, if the farmer and his dog hadn't come along to rescue the herd. It appeared that some stranger had left a gate open and the cows had merrily trouped out selecting our van as a suitable focal point. We made up the time we had lost, and I reflected as we went about our duties, that life on a mobile library was certainly interesting, there was always an adventure round the corner.

A day or two later, in the village of Brinscall, Mrs Buckingham-Jones, a middle-aged, rather erratic personality who thought herself a cut above everyone else in the village, (just because she had a daily help) breezed into the van. She looked absolutely hideous in a pair of striped purple pants, which stretched tightly over her ample behind and made it look more prodigious than ever. As she marched purposefully towards the bookshelves, I detected one or two sniggers from readers already in the van choosing their books, who noticed her unfortunate garb. Eventually she chose her books and, as she had them checked out at the desk, began a long narrative about her holiday in Norway, in as loud a voice as possible so that nobody could miss a word. After patiently listening for ten minutes I was relieved when Mrs Savage, her daily help from the village came to the door and said that Mrs Buckingham-Jones was wanted on the telephone. As she left the van, there were general sighs of relief all round.

'Big mouth,' said little Mrs Thorpe, 'always ranting about where she's been and what she has, proper snobbish I call it.'

'Yes,' agreed Mrs Broome, 'always on about her darling Avril, and her preserves, you know.'

She nodded significantly towards the retreating back of Mrs Buckingham-Jones.

This conversation would doubtless have carried on for another fifteen minutes if we hadn't been interrupted by the Vicar, who came and stood before me, blinking mildly and asking if I had a Frances P.

Keyes that his wife hadn't read. I duly obliged, and we left Brinscall and Mrs Buckingham-Jones behind us.

When I went home at night I related my adventures, and described all the amazing characters I had met during the day. My husband and daughter found it hard to believe that anything so mundane as a mobile library could conjure up such a great wealth of interest, but it certainly did.

Mr Tom Murphy outside his grocery store

Chapter Eleven

Goodbye to it all

SEPTEMBER had come again. The hedges were resplendent with scarlet berries and deadly nightshade flowers, the lovely rowan trees once more sported their blood-red harvest for all to see. The blackberries ripened – an exceptionally good year it was for them too, and I picked almost 7 lbs in my lunch hour one day and made blackberry and apple jam.

Autumn for me was, however, tinged with regret this year as I was serving my notice on the Mobile Library. My husband had obtained a promotion in his work, but it meant that we had to move to the Midlands. Much as I was pleased for my husband, I could not help bitterly regretting having to leave the job which had become so dear to me. However, there was nothing else for it but to accept the situation, and I was determined to make the most of my last few weeks.

The readers, bless their hearts, offered sympathy when I told them of my dilemma and said they'd miss me, but this made me feel worse. I knew that I should miss them all, even the old crotchety ones like Farmer Barnes and Miss Rose Smallbone. I would also miss being out and about and seeing my beloved countryside, as we were to move to a large industrial town.

As we travelled along the lanes from village to village, I drank in as much of the scenery as I could; lovely cottage gardens aflame with dahlias and chrysanthemums; the chestnut trees turning a rich gold, and the swallows preparing for their long journey southwards.

One person of whom I had become particularly fond was Mrs Ruth Airey, who kept large kennels for dogs on the outskirts of Tockholes village. She was an extraordinary person, but a very marvellous one too (in my opinion at any rate). She had been widowed in her late twenties and was left with four young children to bring up. In order to earn a living, yet not leave the children, she had with great courage opened the kennels, and although she'd had a rough start, she'd won in the end and now the kennels were a huge success. Not only was she a very capable woman with animals, she was also a much travelled one. As her children grew up, and the business flourished, she began to travel abroad out of the peak season period, and the tales she could tell of Casablanca, Istanbul, Venice, and even Lima in Peru, would earn her a fortune if she ever wrote them down.

In Tockholes, she had the reputation of being as good as the local vet with sick dogs, and certainly she had a way with them. I have seen her re-set the leg of a huge alsation without any trouble. I spent many hours listening to her tales and also, on several evenings, I was invited to see her slides and cine' films of the fascinating places she had visited. Even when I moved to the Midlands, we still exchanged letters.

The days were becoming more chilly and Bill and I ate our dinners in a café when possible, or took hot soup in a flask. We also made use of the village fish and chip shops (when they were open) and Lancashire steak pudding, chips and peas were often the order of the day. On one occasion Bill and I were eating our puddings in a chip shop café when the door swung open and jolted back savagely against the wall. An old tramp entered in a pathetic condition; his coat was ragged and torn, the soles of his shoes were flapping and a dirty grey and holey jumper cuff trailed from the sleeve of his ancient coat. He looked dreadful, thin and grey and haggard. I have no great love for tramps, but somehow or other I felt sorry for this one. He sat down at a table and looked around, seeing me (rather rudely) staring I'm afraid.

'Have you got a hanky Mrs, so's I can wipe me hands?'

I obliged with two large tissues from my bag.

'Will these do?' I asked.

He took them gratefully and wiped his filthy hands and face, then he ordered the usual dinner of fish, chips, peas, tea, bread and butter. As he slowly ate his fare, I eyed him closely and thought he vaguely reminded me of one of my readers, but I couldn't remember which one. Then suddenly I remembered it was our own old 'recluse' Tommy Riley he resembled.

Slowly the tramp ate on, obviously making the most of every mouthful and eyeing us coldly all the time. Suddenly Mrs Donnelly, the café owner, came into the dining room and on spotting the old tramp, let out a shriek of rage.

'How did you get in?' she screamed pointing an accusing finger at him. 'I thought I told you to keep away, I suppose you've no money to pay and you're having no more free meals from me.'

The old tramp looked up at Mrs D pathetically.

'I had to come, I've been so cold and miserable and had no food for two days, I'll pay you when I get some money.'

But Mrs Donnelly was not in a sympathetic mood.

'Out you go,' she ordered 'and don't come near here again, its only because I've got new staff that you got in at all.'

Something inside me felt very sorry for the tramp and to my surprise

I found myself saying to Mrs D, 'Please let him stay and I'll pay for his meal.'

Mrs D, looked at me as if I'd gone crazy, but at the mention of payment, she agreed to let the tramp finish his dinner at any rate.

Rather sceptically she said to me, 'You'll be sorry, you'll get no thanks from him.'

After saying this she retreated to her chip making in the back. The old tramp finished his dinner, then came over and thanked me. On impulse I asked him if he'd a brother called Tommy Riley who lived in Edgworth village. To my surprise, he said he was Tommy's twin brother, but said that he hadn't seen him for years and how was he?

As we left the café, I reflected on how sad it was to have two recluses like that in the same family. On our next visit to the café, Mrs Donnelly told us a long, rambling tale about Ben the tramp and his twin brother Tommy, and of how they frequented the neighbourhood years ago, doing odd jobs for people but getting more and more dirty and lazy until they both eventually became recluses, and Tommy went off to another village.

Hollinshead Terrace at Tockholes were we paused for lunch.

The days passed much too quickly for my liking, my notice was drawing to a close. As we travelled along, I paid particular attention to the countryside and its beauty, the mellowing leaves, tawny bracken, migrating birds, animals making ready to hibernate and the many other sights and sounds which tell us that autumn is on the way. Village cottages now sported the red catoneastea or virginia creeper and in the gardens a few dahlias and chrysanthemums mingled with the michaelmas daisies. A stray squirrel caught my eye, hungrily looking for nuts, darting in and out of the falling leaves and returning to its drey with its captured prize.

Our readers, too, felt the autumn nip and old Mrs Baron exchanged her straw hat for a closely crocheted bonnet and matching shawl. Miss Marigold Mashom sported red tights (with nose and cheeks to match), long fur-lined boots and a green ski-cap complete with bob. The Pentecostal Mission in Abbey Village set up a new notice to entice sinners and repenters in from the cold. It read: 'Come to Church – new central heating system inside'. Obviously the work of the Vicar, who

was trying to increase his flock by a more material method. Bill Burton, the water bailiff of the reservoirs, now sported an ancient thick tweed suit and very battered deer stalker, looking for all the world like a character from the British Museum.

The rosehips brightened the hedgerows and the birds eagerly plucked the scarlet hawthorn berries from the bushes, greedily preparing for the approaching winter, and I began the sad task of saying goodbye to my readers on each day. Many were the humble little presents I received – a pair of hand knitted gloves or mittens, a pot of homemade jam or lemon curd, a cutting from a favourite plant. These and many other items found their way into my basket from my warm-hearted and generous readers. It was all I could do to keep from crying as they came into the van to bid me farewell.

Early autumn crocuses graced the lawn of Honey Hole Cottage, adding a faint hint of purple to the green grass. Miss Marigold Mashom herself appeared at the door of the van, on this, my last visit to her, a bunch of late calendulas and a small pot of honey were in her hands. These she deposited on my desk.

'Just a small token for your services,' she said softly.

I thanked her and turned away choked with emotion.

On my last visit to Mrs Bilton, as we bumped over the rough farm track, I remembered the blizzard last winter and how we had got stuck there. Mrs Bilton obviously remembered too, for she remarked as she bade me farewell, 'I hope the next librarian keeps to the track this winter.'

Mrs Morton, and her baby daughter, now a bonny bouncing child with the loveliest blue eyes you ever saw, came to the van and wished me good luck, and Mrs Dooley gave me a present of a handwoven scarf, very gay in red and purple which I didn't think I would have the courage to wear. However, I appreciated her thought and thanked her warmly for the present.

Really, all the kindness was a little too much for me and I had a job to control my emotions. Bill and I had our last lunch together by the side of the reservoirs and as I gazed for the last time at their intrinsic beauty, I resolved to return and visit them whenever we came north again.

And so, on the very last day of September, I did my last trek around the villages with Bill. Months later, in the prison of the industrial Midlands, I looked back with nostalgia to the very happy days I had spent during my 'Lancashire Year' and to all the interesting and wonderful people who had become my friends during that short time.